MINI HOOP EMBROIDERIES

OVER 60 LITTLE MASTERPIECES TO STITCH AND WEAR

by Sonia Lyne of

dandelyne™

SEARCH PRESS

CONTENTS

INTRODUCTION 6

TOOL KIT 8

♡ CRAFT SUPPLIES 8

♡ FABRICS & THREAD 11

VARIATIONS 14

GETTING STARTED 16

♡ TRANSFERRING YOUR DESIGNS 16

♡ THE STITCHES 18

♡ DANDE TIPS & TRICKS 20

FRAMING YOUR MINI HOOPS 22

♡ MASTERPIECE FRAMING 22

♡ DECORATE & DISPLAY 26

MINI MASTERPIECES 28

ACKNOWLEDGEMENTS 94

INTRODUCTION

Hello, beautiful hoopie friends. Welcome to my little Dande-world of miniature embroidery hoop bliss. I am thrilled that you are here and that, most importantly, you are about to indulge with me in the wonderful craft that is embroidery… in miniature.

My little hoops were created out of a strong desire to wear my own handiwork, loud and proud. (I am also known to have a short attention span, so the idea of stitching smaller projects was a very attractive idea indeed.) Prior to the creation of my hoops, there were many times where I was so proud of what I had stitched that I wanted to show everyone (there were also times when I wanted to throw them out), and I searched high and low for miniature embroidery hoops so I could adorn every outfit and show off my craftiness (pun intended). I found nothing suitable, so I thought to myself… if I want miniature embroidery hoops, there must be others that want them too. It was at that moment a light bulb lit brightly in my mind's eye and the birth of Dandelyne™ miniature embroidery hoops began. I have not looked back since.

As soon as I think about embroidery, a little warm, fuzzy feeling starts to blossom from my core. It then spreads through my body like a needle gliding through fabric and eventually hits my skin in the form of goose-bumps. Bliss begins. A passionate embroiderer? Yes! It is my retreat, my self-indulgence, my joy, my yoga, my sanity, my inspiration, my creativity, my place to dream. It gives me a sense of belonging to something bigger than I can comprehend. Sounds terrific, huh? It really is! Have you felt this, and more? I really want this for you too!

The 'simple' task of choosing a design to stitch, and which stitch to use from the vast array of stitches that you can choose from, can be very overwhelming. A blank canvas can be inspirational for some and a daunting experience for many. I tend to view the world in stitches; with my mini hoop glasses on I can be standing in the line at a supermarket, eyeing up the strategically placed chocolates, and see a delicious mini masterpiece design just waiting to be stitched. I am ecstatic to have this opportunity to present the ideas that have been bubbling away in my mind for years. When I began writing this book, it was imperative that I felt proud of every single design because, ultimately, I am sharing my heart. This is my heart in a book… for you.

In sharing my passion, designs, tips and tricks, it is my hope that you can feel my excitement and encouragement for every stitch that you do (including the unpicked ones). I would love for you to choose a design that tickles your fancy, whether you are just starting out, are re-igniting a once-loved skill or are a professional stitcher flicking through the pages. If you think it is perfect as is, then dive in. If you are looking at the design and want to change the colours, try different stitches or add extra design features… do it! In fact, I encourage you to experiment, add your flair and, most importantly, enjoy the process from start to finish. Then, once you have stitched one, choose another and another and another… she says, with a big cheesy grin. Dandelyne™ is all about small-scale embroidery projects that are satisfying, rewarding, soul boosting and, frankly, look just so darn cute.

It's time – let's do this! Get ready to be motivated, excited and inspired to stitch up a sea of mini masterpieces that you can be super proud of and show off, or (if you're feeling generous) gift to a loved one.

Smiles,

Sonia Tot

(a.k.a. Mini Hoop Motivator)

TOOL KIT

CRAFT SUPPLIES

One of the many things that I love about embroidery is that your tool kit will not cost the world. That is, unless you are like me and a trip to the craft store to get just one item ends in you bringing home twenty because you 'really, really need' them. Honestly though, a couple of embroidery needles, some fabric, threads in your favourite colours, scissors and an embroidery hoop, and you're all set to go. And, to top it off, all of this can fit in a cute little pencil case or sewing kit so that you can take your stitching anywhere.

Let's take a look at my go-to tools, including options, so that you can head to the store with a check list, or pull out that inherited stash of goodies and start stitching as soon as possible.

NEEDLES

My go-to needles are John James embroidery needles in sizes 1 and 5. Size 1 is the largest size and I use this when I am working with four to six strands of thread. I will use a size 5 needle when I am using one to three strands of thread.

Needles are an essential item for embroidery, and finding a needle that suits your style of stitching is a fun thing to explore and test. They do vary in quality between brands. I find that I am heavy handed when I stitch, and some needles tend to bend easily when I work with them. The most important thing is that your needle has a sharp point to pierce through your fabric with ease. The three types of needles that I have in my tool kit are:

♡ **Embroidery (also called crewel) needles** – sharp tip and a large eye

♡ **Chenille needles** – sharp tip and a large eye (but larger in length in comparison to embroidery needles)

♡ **Tapestry needle** – blunt tip and a large eye; great for working with open weave fabrics such as hessian or lace.

I encourage you to try a few varieties and brands, and find the ones that work for you.

EMBROIDERY HOOPS

Oh, I love embroidery hoops, and the range that is available is vast. The purpose of an embroidery hoop is to keep your fabric taut while you are stitching, like the skin of a drum. Using a hoop throughout will result in your stitches resting perfectly in your fabric at the end; working without one can lead to uneven stitches and tension. You will find that there are circle, oval and square hoop designs; they also come in a range of sizes and in wood and plastic options too. There is so much on offer, and the type and size you use will be a personal choice and depend on the project that you are working on.

An **8cm (3in) wooden embroidery hoop** is my size of choice when designing and stitching for my mini embroideries, and it is the one that I have used for working all of the designs in this book.

And lastly... not to forget the **Dandelyne™ miniature embroidery hoop**. There are **seven hoop sizes** in the Dandelyne™ family that you can choose from. The purpose of the Dande-hoops are to frame your handiwork, and wear your stitchy awesomeness loud and proud. They are the original (since 2011) and the best.

SCISSORS

♡ **Snips** for cutting embroidery threads.

♡ **Dressmaking shears/scissors** for cutting fabric only. (Sure, go ahead and use my fabric scissors on paper, said no-one ever.)

♡ **All-purpose scissors** for cutting paper, interfacing, etc.

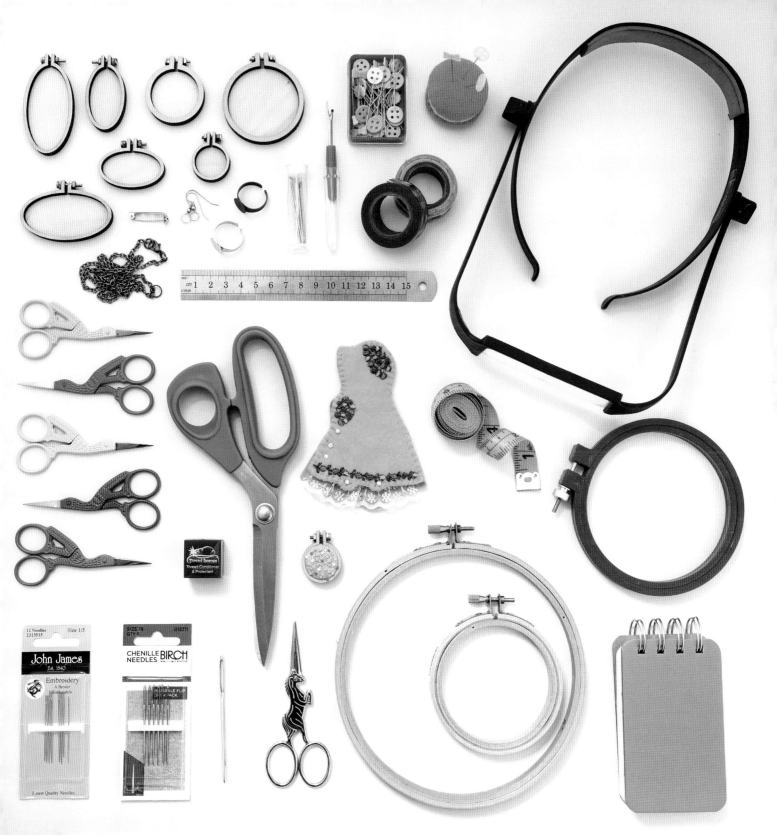

TRANSFER TOOLS

These are shown and discussed in greater detail on pages 16 to 17.

- ♡ **HB pencil**
- ♡ **Eraser**
- ♡ **Carbon paper**
- ♡ **Fabric pens** – water soluble and air erasable
- ♡ **Light box** (or window)
- ♡ **Water soluble stabilizers**

TOOLS FOR FRAMING YOUR DANDELYNE™ MINI HOOPS

These are shown and discussed in greater detail on pages 22–25.

- ♡ **Dandelyne™ miniature embroidery hoop kit**
- ♡ **Small flat-head screwdriver** (or butter knife)
- ♡ **Pliers** (or tweezers)
- ♡ **Pencil or pen**
- ♡ **Craft or wood glue**
- ♡ **Hot glue gun and glue**
- ♡ **Fabric scissors**
- ♡ **Bull clips/clamps** (or heavy book)

GOODIES I LOVE TO HAVE ON HAND

- ♡ **Tape measure and ruler**
- ♡ **Quick unpick/seam ripper** This is an essential item in my eyes because there are times when I have unpicked more stitches than I have sewn. If I am unable to locate my quick unpick, using the eye end of the needle does the trick.
- ♡ **Pins** Great to have on hand when you need to keep extra elements of a design in place.
- ♡ **Washi tape** Useful when following the light box/window method of transferring (see page 17), and also for holding threads in a position while you are working on different elements of a design.
- ♡ **Notebook** For recording ideas.
- ♡ **Magnifying glasses** I wear glasses, and I take it up a notch by wearing magnifying glasses too. I call them my goggles. My family laugh at me when I wear them, but then I show off my skills and I get the last laugh! You can also get lights with magnifiers in them, when you want to take your tool kit up a level.
- ♡ **Thread conditioner** When I am feeling fancy and working on extra-special projects, I love to use this so that my threads are extra smooth. I use both 'Thread Heaven' and beeswax, depending upon my mood.
- ♡ **Needle minders** Keeping your needles safe from the sides of couches and off the floor is definitely something to think about. I love to use my needle minder while stitching, as it has a little magnet hidden inside which your needles stick to. It is super handy to have on the side as you work a project. Alternatively, I always have my little macaroon pin cushion on hand so that I have a choice of needles readily available. If I have any extra embroidery needles, or if I have too many about, I will transfer them to my handmade needle case (a little hooded girl design made of felt, stitched for me by a woman I fondly call 'Mum').

DANDE TIP

My lovely needle minder was made by the wonderful Hello Floss (Instagram @madebyliss). You can find her minders via her linked Etsy shop and BrynnandCo, among others.

FABRICS & THREAD

'Exciting' and 'overwhelming' are the two words that come to mind when I think about choosing fabrics and thread for my embroidery projects. There are times when you will know exactly what you want, and other times when you are paralyzed to start because you feel overstimulated by the fabric options available. Oh, and then there are colour choices to be made too. A big deep breath, and taking the time to peruse the web for inspiration, can work wonders.

Colour! I love it, and lots of it. I tend to want to include too many colours in my projects and I have trouble eliminating some. To assist in my colour choices and to tone things down, I will often head to Instagram and check out Jessica Colaluca @designseeds: there, photographs of everyday scenes inspire colour palettes, and Jessica then pairs up these images with six colour swatches. I also regularly use colour-grab apps, such as ColourFinder and Dulux Visualizer. These allow you to use your own photos to pick out the colour palette. The 'browse' section of the Dulux app is particularly handy for looking at tones and hues. If all else fails, I will head to my thread stash, choose five of my favourite colours and take it from there.

So, let's take a look at some of the fabric and thread options available. Over the page is a list of my favourites and some handy tips to help you choose.

FABRICS

- **Quilting cotton** is my number one choice. A good quality quilting cotton, such as the Kona brand, is nice and strong and the weave is just lovely to stitch. The big bonus of quilting cotton is the vast selection of colours available.

- **Calico** is cheap! It is a woven fabric that is made from unbleached, not fully processed cotton. It will often have little husks in the weave, giving it a raw and natural look.

- **Linen** is absolutely divine to stitch with. It is durable, textural and luxurious. It comes in a variety of weights: light, medium and heavy. It can also have a loose or tight weave.

- **Printed cotton** is similar to quilting cotton in that you have a HUGE amount of choice. Using a printed background can give your design a whole new look.

- **Felt** is readily available, comes in oodles of colours and is made of wool, acrylic or a blend of the two. It is fun to stitch on and it doesn't fray. It is also terrific as a feature in designs, using stitches or glue to secure it. Wool felt is my preferred choice.

- **Tulle, netting and sheer fabrics** can be associated with wedding dresses, fancy gowns and costumes. The see-through element means that your design will pop in a whole new light. I would suggest mastering a few basic stitches first, and then indulge and experiment with these types of fabrics.

- **Light-weight hessian** is made from jute and has an open weave, lending itself to thicker thread options and embellishments. It is available in much heavier weights, but for the purpose of framing your design in a Dandelyne™ miniature embroidery hoop I would strongly advise using only this lighter type, as the thicker weight would be too much for a little Dande-hoop.

- **Vintage cotton and lace** Upcycling op shop (charity or thrift shop) finds and giving them a whole new life is an inexpensive and great option for your projects. It can also be a wonderful starting point as many pieces are already adorned with designs.

- **Light-weight Aida** is a much-loved fabric of choice for cross-stitch designs. It is similar to hessian when it comes to the weights that are available. Again, the thicker weight will be too much for a little Dande-hoop, so I recommend using a lighter type.

THREAD

- **Six-stranded embroidery thread** is the most common thread used for embroidery it and comes in an enormous range of colours. You will invest in a skein of embroidery thread that can be separated into six strands (hence the name). I like to use the range by DMC, and it is their range I have used throughout the book, but feel free to use whichever brand you have to hand.

- **Perle cotton** is a single-stranded twisted thread, and it will give your design a slightly raised look (with a twist).

- **Metallic embroidery thread** is a single-stranded thread and can be used to create some sparkle in your designs.

- **Neon** I am a fan of the Light Effects range from DMC. It has six strands, just like the regular embroidery thread, but the difference is that it is 100 per cent polyester and is more slippery to work with. I would recommend practising with one strand at first, to get a feel for it.

- **Wool** For a feature in your embroidery designs or as a whole design, wool is super fun to work with. You can use tapestry wool, crewel wool or just some wool you have lying around from knitting or crochet projects.

TRIMS & FUN BITS

An embroidered design is not limited by its stitches. No, no, no. You can add fun, crafty trims and accessories to give your design an extra dimension and texture. Things like, but not limited to:

- **Beads**
- **Sequins**
- **Ribbon**
- **Cord**
- **Buttons**

VARIATIONS ▶▶▶

When you dive into the designs later in this book with the knowledge of the variety of fabrics and threads available, I want you to open your beautiful, creative mind and think about how they can be stitched or celebrated in different ways. A new stitch, thread or fabric choice can completely transform a design. PLAY, EXPERIMENT, INDULGE and, most importantly, ENJOY!

1 Reverse chain stitch, secured with two back stitches, using one strand of metallic thread on tulle

2 Couch stitch (puffed) using tapestry wool on cotton

3 Cross stitch on linen

4 Satin stitch using variegated perle cotton on calico

5 Original design from 'Simplicity' project (see pages 30–32) – reverse chain stitch on cotton

6 Blanket stitch felt heart on felt

7 Back stitch and straight stitches on light denim

8 Whipped back stitch using black perle cotton (back stitch) and one strand of white six-stranded embroidery thread (whipped) on printed cotton

9 Couch stitch using metallic thread on leather cord, on a light-weight hessian print fabric

GETTING STARTED

TRANSFERRING YOUR DESIGNS

Alright, so you have your design ready and you have chosen your fabric and threads; you're now ready to stitch. Nearly. Let's look at the ways you can transfer your design onto your fabric. I have always been a big fan of using my window as a light box and tracing with an HB pencil. I still do this at times, but recently I was introduced to a method that I call the 'game-changer'. My gorgeous friend Alison from The Quilt Shop showed me how I could transfer my designs using a photocopier and spray adhesive. I am so excited to share this with you so let's start with this method first.

MY FAVOURITE METHOD

SPRAY & PRINT METHOD OR 'GAME-CHANGER'

YOU WILL NEED:

- Temporary spray adhesive for fabric (I love the 505 Spray & Fix)
- A4 (8⅓ x 11¾in) size sheet of card
- Chosen fabric, cut to A4 (8⅓ x 11¾in) size
- Design ready to print
- Printer/photocopier (both inkjet and laser copiers will do the trick. Please note: most printers/copiers can handle fabric in the following way, but always check the manufacturer's handbook first.)

INSTRUCTIONS:

1 Spray the piece of card as per the spray can instructions. I like to spray the outer edges first and then fill in the centre. A light, even spray across the card is perfect. Too much and it will get soggy.

2 Place your A4 (8⅓ x 11¾in) piece of fabric on top of the card. Line it up with your card on one side and then smooth it over the rest of the card. You will be able to lift it off and replace if there are too many wrinkles. You want it flat and smooth, just like paper.

3 Insert your 'fabric paper' into the rear feeder of your printer/photocopier.

4 Upload your design on your computer, either by scanning from this book or using an existing picture in your folder, and set it up to print. Press the PRINT button.

5 Smile like a Cheshire cat as you watch your perfectly printed design ease out. Peel the fabric off your card, and you're all set to go!

OTHER OPTIONS

CARBON PAPER & PENCIL METHOD

YOU WILL NEED:

- Carbon paper – available in black or white (for darker fabrics) and you can grab this from most stationery stores
- HB pencil and eraser

INSTRUCTIONS:

Place your fabric on a table, carbon paper on top (dark side down). Position your design on top and trace over the top with your HB pencil **(1)**. You are then ready to stitch over the printed design **(2)**. Simple and effective.

1

2

LIGHT BOX OR WINDOW METHOD

YOU WILL NEED:

- Light box or window
- HB pencil and eraser

INSTRUCTIONS:

Using either a light box or window, secure your design to the surface with a strip of washi tape. Position your fabric on top and again, secure with washi tape. Oh, that washi tape comes in handy for so many different things, doesn't it? Then, trace your design with an HB pencil. I like to sketch it softly, so that if I make a mistake I can use an eraser to gently rub it out.

WARNING

Using an eraser can upset the fabric, so please use it gently to avoid this.

FABRIC PEN METHOD

YOU WILL NEED:

- Fabric pens – water soluble or air erasable

INSTRUCTIONS:

With a water soluble or air erasable pen, simply draw your design onto the fabric; then, when you have finished stitching, wash it off with water.

There are lots of fabric pen brands. Personally, I love an air erasable pen; the ink just disappears. There have been occasions it has not cleared completely, so my tip is to use a cotton bud dipped in a small amount of water and gently rub out the pen mark.

Fabric pens come in a variety of colours too which is handy when working on printed fabrics and darker colours. Sublime Stitching (www.sublimestitching.com) has a fantastic selection of transfer materials for you to choose from.

WATER SOLUBLE PENCIL
クロバー チャコペル 「水溶性」

AIR ERASABLE PEN
Ink is nontoxic & soluble, can be removed by soapy water

⁝ THE STITCHES ⁝

I have oodles of embroidery books and I could peruse their pages all day long, looking at the vast array of stitches available – they're like my gossip mags (without anything gossipy). Let's look at my go-to stitches, and the ones that I have used for the designs throughout this book.

STRAIGHT STITCH

Similar to running stitch but you can stitch anywhere your heart desires. Your stitches can be worked to any length and at any angle.

RUNNING STITCH

Weave in and out to create a snazzy dashed line.

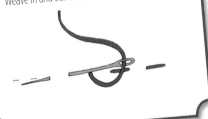

BACK STITCH

I use this stitch often for outlines. Instead of moving forwards you will be heading back into the end of the previous stitch, filling all the gaps and creating a sweet, unbroken line of stitches.

REVERSE CHAIN STITCH (A PERSONAL FAVOURITE)

Chain stitch is more commonly used but reverse chain has a similar effect, although worked in a slightly different way. I find this method easier, and it is the one that I use throughout the book. Swooping your needle under each previous chain is simply fun.

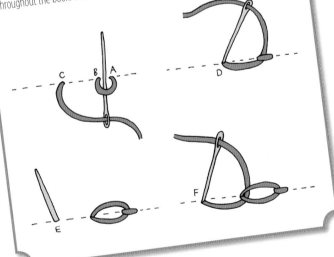

DETACHED CHAIN STITCH

This variation of chain stitch allows you to create cute individual looped stitches, commonly used for flower petals. If you work detached chain stitches into a circle it is known as lazy daisy stitch.

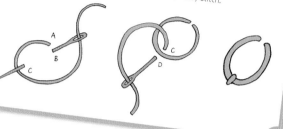

SATIN STITCH

This is a beautiful filling stitch that allows you to 'colour' in your designs. You will be stitching close together, in parallel lines.

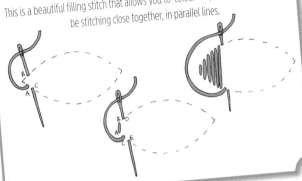

COUCHING STITCH

The possibilities with this versatile stitch are huge. You can create thin lines, bold, textural lines and anything in between.

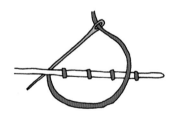

SPIDER WEB STITCH

Oh, this stitch will tickle your fancy, I am certain of it. There is more weaving involved then stitching, and the end result speaks for itself. Superb!

FRENCH KNOT STITCH

A stitch that resembles a tiny bead. If they are worked closely together they sure do pack a pop, and when worked individually they are a gorgeous highlight in any design.

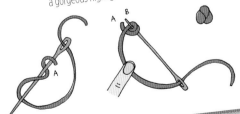

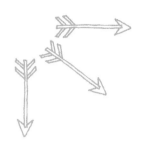
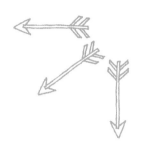

DANDE TIPS & TRICKS

Have you flicked through the pages and now you're keen to start stitching a mini masterpiece? Ooh, I wonder what design you have chosen? Before you begin, let's look at a few handy tips to ensure all bases are covered, and I'll share with you a few tricks that I have learnt on my embroidery journey.

HOOP & FABRIC SIZE

My choice of hoop for initially stitching all the designs in this book is an 8cm (3in) wooden embroidery hoop. For each project you will need to cut a piece of fabric that measures approx. 13cm (5in) square. It can be a square or circle, just make sure you leave enough fabric so that you can pull it taut around your hoop. You don't need to worry about cutting straight edges for your fabric, as you will be trimming off the excess to frame your mini masterpiece in a Dandelyne™ mini hoop later.

HOW TO MAKE A HOOP FABRIC SANDWICH

Loosen the screw at the top of the hoop, turning it anti-clockwise to release the inner ring. Place your fabric on top of the inner ring. Grab your outer ring and place it on top, pressing it firmly in place. Slightly turn the screw at the top clockwise to secure your fabric; then, moving around the hoop, pull on the excess fabric to get your fabric sitting taut in the frame. One last tighten of the screw and you're ready to go.

SPLITTING YOUR EMBROIDERY THREAD

You have six strands to have fun with, and you can use one or all, or anything in between, depending on the look you are after. If you choose to split your threads, you will need to first separate them at one end into the number of strands you desire, and then slowly pull them apart.

You may find with this method that it tangles easily at the base. To help sort this out, you can pop the base in your mouth, purse your lips together to hold the thread, and then continue to pull it apart. (This method is not always regarded as the correct way but many of us do it *wink wink*.)

Carefully separate your strands with your fingertip.

Select one strand.

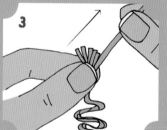

Hold the bunch with one hand, and pull your chosen strand.

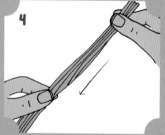

Pull the remaining threads down, and repeat for remaining strands.

TIPS FOR WORKING WITH YOUR THREAD

Thread before you begin You can be extra prepared for your stitchy session by having your needles all threaded up with the colours for your project. Personally, I love having a little display of needles and threads in front of me so that I can swap between colours easily. Then, I can just pick up and stitch.

Where to pull the thread from the skein A skein is generally wrapped in two labels. One is larger in width. Find the end of the thread, which is usually hanging loose, and gently pull it from the skein, holding the smaller label.

Length of thread I like to use my fingertip to elbow as a guide for cutting a length of approx. 50cm (20in). I am always tempted to cut a longer length of thread and I always pay for it... in knots.

STARTING & FINISHING

There are two methods you can use.

Waste knot Tie a knot at the end of your thread and, on the top, insert your needle into the fabric. Start stitching a little further along the line or area of your design, moving back towards your starting point with each stitch. When you reach your knot, cut it off. Once you've completed your design, end your work by working two small back stitches and cutting off the remaining thread.

TOP OF
FABRIC

Weaving Leave a length of thread approx. 10cm (4in) when you begin stitching, and then weave it back through once you've worked a few stitches. Snip off the excess thread. You will also end your embroidery this way, once you've finished stitching the design.

BACK OF
FABRIC

THE PERFECT FINISH

Use the weave of fabric as a guide This is something that I do often. It really helps keep the shape of a design consistent. To work a simple straight line, follow the crosswise threads in the fabric (the weft) to produce a perfect line.

Snip your threads as you go I find snipping your threads, especially when you change colours, stops them from getting caught up in the stitches ahead.

Pull out knots gently Knots do happen, and often this can be because the thread has slowly begun to twist as you work, or, simply, it just does. I have learnt that, rather than pulling harder and tightening the knot, if you stop as you see it happening you can easily return it to a single thread by gently and slowly opening the thread on both sides of the knot. This will unravel it (and it is actually quite satisfying when you do it). There are those occasions when a knot will just stay a knot. At these times, take a deep breath... and snip it off. Weave the thread back through your stitches in the same way you'd finish for the weaving method opposite, and then re-thread and keep going.

Unpicked holes For those stitches you've had to unpick, tickle the fabric from behind with your fingernail to readjust the weave of the fabric back to its original state. It will look like it was never there.

Measuring trick for accurate stitch lengths Place a length of masking tape approx. 5cm (2in) long on the outer edge of your thumb. Now, use a ruler and pen to mark your desired stitch length along the tape. Then, you can use this as a guide as you stitch. There you have a 'rule of thumb' tip!

FRAMING YOUR MINI HOOPS ▷▷

MASTERPIECE FRAMING

It's time! You get to frame your stitchy awesomeness and show it off. No more words – just pure excitement. Let's dive in.

YOU WILL NEED:

- ✿ Dandelyne™ miniature embroidery hoop kit
- ✿ Your 'mini masterpiece' (stitched design)
- ✿ Small flat-head screwdriver (or butter knife)
- ✿ Pliers (or tweezers)
- ✿ Pencil, pen or air erasable/water soluble pen
- ✿ Craft or wood glue
- ✿ Hot glue gun
- ✿ Fabric scissors
- ✿ Bull clips or clamps (or heavy book)
- ✿ A treat of your choice to enjoy while the glue dries...

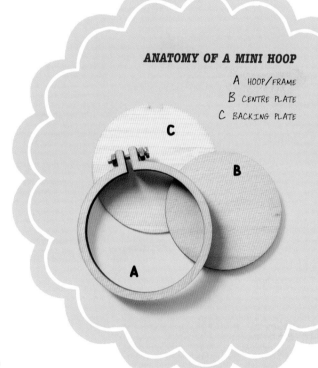

ANATOMY OF A MINI HOOP

A HOOP/FRAME
B CENTRE PLATE
C BACKING PLATE

❊ HOT DANDE TIP ❊

The hot glue gun does not always play nice. It can burn. Take care when using it. If it is your first time using one, you may want to put sticking plasters (band-aids) on the tips of your fingers to avoid hot glue on your skin. Ye-ouch!

INSTRUCTIONS:

1 Grab the nuts and screw (bolt) from your Dandelyne™ mini hoop set. Fasten one nut to the screw, all the way to the top.

2 Insert the screw through the top of the hoop.

3 Fasten the second nut onto the screw. It doesn't need to be tight. You want to leave a little space so that the hoop fits easily over your design.

4 Place your mini hoop on your stitched mini masterpiece. Position it so it frames your design exactly as you would like to see it. You can play around to make it central, or not. With either a pencil, pen or air erasable/water soluble pen, draw a cutting line approx. 7–10mm (¼–⅜in) around the hoop. The extra fabric will be glued to the back of the centre plate.

5 Loosen the screw on your larger embroidery hoop and release your mini masterpiece. Now, cut it out.

6 Grab your centre plate and place your design on top. Then, place the miniature hoop over the top and push down to secure the design into position. You may need to do this a couple of times, re-positioning your design to get it just right.

7 Flip it over and with the hot glue gun squeeze a line of glue around the edge of the centre plate.

8 Push the excess fabric down onto your centre plate, moving in one direction around the edge of the hoop. Keep pressing and smoothing the fabric in the hoop while the glue is still warm to ensure a flat and gorgeous-looking design.

9 Now tighten the final nut on your mini hoop a little (you can use your finger for this step) then, using your flat-head screwdriver or butter knife, tighten it a little more. You want it to be secure in the frame. **Be careful not to over tighten.**

10 Grab your backing plate and squeeze a line of craft or wood glue around the edge. You're nearly there. Exciting!

11 Position the backing plate onto the back of your hoop, with the notch top and centre. Use bull clips, clamps or a heavy book to help keep it secure and dry tight.

12 Treat time. WOOT WOOT! Leave it to dry as per the instructions on your glue. Once your mini hoop is dry you can then turn it into a necklace, brooch, earring, keyring or even a crown. That is 100 per cent up to you.

> VOILÀ… your mini masterpiece is complete. It's time to wear it loud and proud. Air high fives!

BROOCHES

Personally, I love industrial strength glue (such as E6000 glue). Position your brooch back closer to the top of the hoop so when you wear it all of the weight is at the top of the hoop and your brooch mini masterpiece will sit perfectly on your outfit.

ATTACHING OTHER HARDWARE

If you want to make a necklace, keyring or anything that requires a connection to the top section of the hoop, you will need to use your pliers to unfasten the nut so you can slot the ring/connection in the middle.

DECORATE & DISPLAY

Framing your mini masterpieces isn't the end of the story – oh no.
Have fun decorating your mini hoops and then display them in a myriad
of ways for ultimate hoopie goodness.

DECORATE

♡ **Paint your hoops to highlight your designs**   There is a vast price range when it comes to acrylic paints; I have found the cheap ones work well with a couple of coats.

♡ **Wrap your hoop frame** in ribbon, adhesive fabric tape, bias binding or wool. You can also use the wrapped pieces as an anchor point for tassels and trims.

♡ **Use glitter** (and glue) to make them sparkle and pop.

♡ **Use nail polish** to create a glossy and colourful look.

♡ **Embellish them with tiny beads**.

♡ **Use washi tape** on the outer rim for a subtle effect.

DISPLAY

You can wear your mini masterpieces loud and proud and you can also have them on display to be adored. Here are a few ideas that you can have fun with.

- ♡ Stick **a self-adhesive hook** on your wall and hang your necklaces up.

- ♡ **There are miniature easels and canvasses available**. You can fasten your mini masterpieces to the canvas to create a stunning miniature display. Jazz up the canvas with paint or wrap it in patterned paper or fabric to create a background that will highlight your design.

- ♡ **Create a mobile of mini hoops**, or even a wall hanging.

- ♡ **Pop them into picture frames**, old or new.

THE MINI MASTERPIECES ▶▶▶

Here we go! Before you dive into the treasure trove of circular goodness, there are a few important details you'll need to know.

MATERIALS

For every project you will need:

- 🌸 Fabric scissors
- 🌸 Snips, for threads
- 🌸 Size 5 embroidery needle, unless stated otherwise
- 🌸 Six-stranded embroidery thread (see individual designs for DMC colours), unless stated otherwise
- 🌸 8cm (3in) embroidery hoop to stitch in initially, before framing your design in the mini hoops – you can use a larger hoop if you prefer

Additional or alternative materials needed for individual designs are provided next to each photographed hoop.

TEMPLATES & STITCH GUIDES

Lots of the mini masterpieces include templates and/or stitch guides, and these will appear close to each photographed hoop. These are all to scale (100 per cent in size).

Before you begin stitching, I recommend transferring the stitch guides onto your fabric. For ease, trace/scan/photocopy them onto a piece of paper and cut them out with paper scissors – do not use your fabric scissors! To transfer a design/stitch guide, follow a method on pages 16 to 17 that works for you.

Some of the stitch guides include numbers, to help you see where and in what order to start stitching. These do not need to be transferred to the fabric.

EXAMPLE OF STITCH GUIDE

FRAMING YOUR HOOP

Once your design is finished, you'll be instructed to frame up your hoop. To do this, assemble the tools and follow the instructions detailed on pages 22–25. It will be assumed that these tools are beside you as you work your mini masterpiece.

SIMPLICITY

Let's start with that universal symbol – a heart. 'What's not to love?' she says, with a big cheesy grin. We'll second that emotion in stitch, and in doing so illuminate the different effects that it can have.

THREE-ROW HEART

MATERIALS:

❀ Fabric, for your base – I have used quilting cotton in duck egg
❀ 5.5cm (2¼in) Dandelyne™ miniature embroidery hoop

SUGGESTED STITCHES:

❀ Back stitch

DMC COLOURS:

958

INSTRUCTIONS:

1 Secure your base fabric with transferred design in your 8cm (3in) embroidery hoop and get ready to stitch.

2 Use back stitches to create your heart. Start with the outer heart, using four strands of thread; followed by the middle heart, using two strands; finally, end with the inner heart, using one strand.

3 Three-Row Heart complete! Frame your mini masterpiece.

STITCH GUIDE

3
2
1

❀ DANDE TIP ❀

Revisit pages 14 to 15 to see the variations that you can create with one simple graphic.

CHALLENGE: Use one of your favourite stitches, a favourite fabric and a favourite thread colour, and stitch a little heart just for you.

RUNNING STITCH HEART

MATERIALS:

- Fabric, for your base – I have used quilting cotton in cornflower blue
- 2.5cm (1in) Dandelyne™ miniature embroidery hoop

SUGGESTED STITCHES:

- Running stitch

DMC COLOURS:

809

INSTRUCTIONS:

1 Secure your base fabric with transferred design in your 8cm (3in) embroidery hoop and get ready to stitch.

2 Work running stitches for the entire design. You can start working from either side. I have used two strands of thread.

3 Running Stitch Heart complete! Frame your mini masterpiece.

STITCH GUIDE

REVERSE CHAIN HEART

MATERIALS:

- Fabric, for your base – I have used quilting cotton in mint
- 4cm (1½in) Dandelyne™ miniature embroidery hoop

SUGGESTED STITCHES:

- Reverse chain stitch

DMC COLOURS:

3609

INSTRUCTIONS:

1 Secure your base fabric with transferred design in your 8cm (3in) embroidery hoop and get ready to stitch.

2 Work reverse chain stitches to create your heart, starting from the bottom right-hand side. I have used two strands of thread.

3 Reverse Chain Heart complete! Frame your mini masterpiece.

STITCH GUIDE

SPIDER WEB FLOWERS

Ooooh la la! A woven spider web, in thread, transforms into the most divine little embroidered flower. Agree? This little stitch has become ever so popular within the embroidery community and, personally, it ticks all of the boxes for me too. It is simple to do and the effect is stunning. If this is your first time doing the spider web stitch, I know that you will be 'oohing' and 'ahhing' as you create your very own.

Are you ready? Let's do it.

GARDEN

MATERIALS:

❀ Fabric, for the base – I have used quilting cotton in mustard
❀ Large 6.2 x 3.4cm (2½ x 1⅜in) horizontal oval Dandelyne™ miniature embroidery hoop

SUGGESTED STITCHES:

❀ Back stitch
❀ Detached chain stitch
❀ French knots
❀ Spider web stitch

DMC COLOURS:

554, 958, 964, 3608, 3842

INSTRUCTIONS:

1 Secure your base fabric with transferred design in your 8cm (3in) embroidery hoop, and get ready to stitch.

2 Use back stitch for the stems of the flowers and detached chain stitch for the leaves. I have used two strands of thread for both. I like to stitch the leaves as I am working the back stitch; alternatively, you can stitch the leaves once you have finished stitching the stems.

3 Spider web time. YAY! I have used two strands of thread for each flower. In addition, I have used two colours for each flower by either adding a French knot in the middle, once the spider web stitch is complete, or changing the thread colour half way (see picture below). Use the photograph as a reference for colour changes.

4 Garden complete! Frame your mini masterpiece.

STITCH GUIDE

DANDE TIP

Spider web stitch is SO satisfying. Now that you have mastered the technique I encourage you to try it with different types of threads for a whole new look. Try wool, variegated thread, perle cotton, ribbon (yes, ribbon) and metallic threads. Oh, the possibilities!

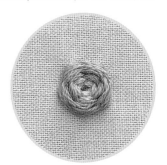

MIXED-COLOUR
SPIDER WEB ROSE

LOVE HEART

MATERIALS:

❀ Fabric, for the base – I have used quilting cotton in hot pink

❀ 5.5cm (2¼in) Dandelyne™ miniature embroidery hoop

SUGGESTED STITCHES:

❀ Spider web stitch

❀ Straight stitch

DMC COLOURS:

353, 602, 977, 3341, 3708

INSTRUCTIONS:

1 Secure your base fabric with transferred design in your 8cm (3in) embroidery hoop, and get ready to stitch.

2 Work straight stitch for the lines surrounding the heart, using the photograph as a reference for colour changes. I have used two strands of thread.

3 Now it's time to stitch those gorgeous rosettes. I have used two strands of thread for each flower. Work multiple different-size spider web stitches to create five sweet flowers.

4 Love Heart complete! Frame your mini masterpiece.

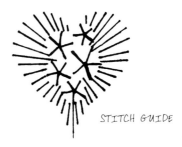

STITCH GUIDE

VINE

MATERIALS:

❀ Fabric, for the base – I have used quilting cotton in ultramarine

❀ Small 2.7 x 4.5cm (1 x 1¾in) vertical oval Dandelyne™ miniature embroidery hoop

SUGGESTED STITCHES:

❀ Detached chain stitch

❀ Spider web stitch

❀ Straight stitch

DMC COLOURS:

727, 958, 964, 977, 3607

INSTRUCTIONS:

1 Secure your base fabric with transferred design in your 8cm (3in) embroidery hoop, and get ready to stitch.

2 Use back stitch, straight stitch and detached chain stitch for the vine stem and leaves. I have used two strands of thread.

3 Flower time. Use spider web stitch to complete the three flowers. I have used four strands of thread for the flower in the middle and two strands of thread for the outer flowers.

4 Vine complete! Frame your mini masterpiece.

STITCH GUIDE

COLOUR & STITCH

This technique will have you smiling from ear to ear. You get to stitch and colour in – oh yes, indeed! And how sweet is the effect?

I have a dream to own an extremely colourful home one day, with a beautiful pink or mint front door. It may be a great feature, or it may make the neighbours think that I'm bonkers. Until then, colourful embroidered houses will have to do. I have used pastel pencils by Derwent for these designs, and I think they have come up a treat, but you can also use fabric pens, fabric paint or regular watercolour paints. Play and experiment for different effects.

HOME

MATERIALS:

- Fabric, for the base – I have used quilting cotton in lilac
- Pastel pencils – I have used yellow, light orange, mint green, pink, magenta and cornflower blue
- 5.5cm (2¼in) Dandelyne™ miniature embroidery hoop

SUGGESTED STITCHES:

- Back stitch
- French knots
- Straight stitch

DMC COLOURS:

Blanc, 602, 727, 809, 954, 977, 3607, 3841

INSTRUCTIONS:

1 Secure your base fabric with transferred design in your 8cm (3in) embroidery hoop, and get ready to stitch.

2 Colour in the house with your pencils or paint and brush, using the photograph as a reference for colour changes.

3 With corresponding colours, use back stitch for the outline of the house. I have used two strands of thread.

4 Use straight stitch for the flower stems and window panes. I have used one strand of thread.

5 Use French knots for the flowers. I have used one strand of thread.

6 Home complete! Frame your mini masterpiece.

STITCH GUIDE

ᕮ DANDE TIP ᕮ

If the colouring fades a little you can always touch it up afterwards, being careful not to colour your stitches – or, you may like to experiment and colour the stitches too. You can use pencils, crayons or paint to achieve very different looks. The effect will be dependant upon the fabric that you are using, so it is important to test them first.

CAMPING IN THE MOUNTAINS

MATERIALS:

❀ Fabric, for the base – I have used quilting cotton in white
❀ Pastel pencils – I have used grey and turquoise
❀ 4cm (1½in) Dandelyne™ miniature embroidery hoop

SUGGESTED STITCHES:

❀ Back stitch
❀ Straight stitch

DMC COLOURS:

Blanc, 415, 727, 840, 977, 3328, 3809

INSTRUCTIONS:

1 Secure your base fabric with transferred design in your 8cm (3in) embroidery hoop, and get ready to stitch.

2 Colour in the tent and mountains with your pencils or paint and brush.

3 With corresponding colours, work back stitch for the outline of the tent and mountains. I have used two strands of thread.

4 Use straight stitch for the fire and logs. I have used two strands of thread.

5 Camping in the Mountains complete! Frame your mini masterpiece.

STITCH GUIDE

BEACH HUTS

MATERIALS:

❀ Fabric, for the base – I have used quilting cotton in cornflower blue
❀ Pastel pencils – I have used yellow, light orange, burnt orange, purple, magenta, teal and turquoise
❀ Large 6.2 x 3.4cm (2½ x 1⅜in) horizontal oval Dandelyne™ miniature embroidery hoop

SUGGESTED STITCHES:

❀ Back stitch
❀ Straight stitch

DMC COLOURS:

Blanc, 415 602, 727, 954, 977, 3607, 3809

INSTRUCTIONS:

1 Secure your base fabric with the transferred design in your 8cm (3in) embroidery hoop, and get ready to stitch.

2 Colour in the huts with your pencils or paint and paint brush, using the photograph as a reference for colour changes.

3 With corresponding colours, work back stitch for the outlines of the huts. I have used one strand of thread for the doorways, and two strands of thread for the rest of the outlines.

4 Use straight stitch for the hut stands. I have used two strands of thread.

5 Beach Huts complete. YAY! Frame your mini masterpiece.

STITCH GUIDE

SUBLIME SATIN STITCH

Sweet, sweet satin stitch fills my heart – and designs – perfectly. The cloud and bunting designs are two of the very first designs that I ever created for Dandelyne™ hoops and I am thrilled to be able to share them with you. The jigsaw is a new addition, and one that I feel is a 'perfect fit'.

See what I did there.

JIGSAW

STITCH GUIDE

MATERIALS:

❀ Fabric, for your base – I have used quilting cotton in white
❀ Large 6.2 x 3.4cm (2½ x 1⅜in) horizontal oval Dandelyne™ miniature embroidery hoop

SUGGESTED STITCHES:

❀ Back stitch
❀ Running stitch
❀ Satin stitch

DMC COLOURS:

415, 3341, 3609

INSTRUCTIONS:

1   Secure your base fabric with transferred design in your 8cm (3in) embroidery hoop, and get ready to stitch.

2   For this design I have stitched the outline of Jigsaw by working back stitch first. This is another technique used to give the design more height, and it also helps keep the design lines neat and tidy. I have used three strands of thread.

3   Work satin stitch to fill the jigsaw pieces. I have used three strands of thread for each colour.

4   Work a single row of running stitches across the jigsaw pieces to connect them. I have used two strands of thread.

5   Jigsaw complete! Frame your mini masterpiece.

> ❧ **DANDE TIP** ❧
>
> When using satin stitch I absolutely love using the weave of the fabric to ensure my parallel stitches are uniform, and that the length of each stitch creates an even line. The weave of the fabric is like a grid and I use it, with my magnifying goggles on, to create straight lines. For curved edges, I will use the grid of the fabric like steps.

BUNTING

MATERIALS:

- Fabric, for your base – I have used quilting cotton in white
- 4cm (1½in) Dandelyne™ miniature embroidery hoop

SUGGESTED STITCHES:

- Back stitch
- Satin stitch

DMC COLOURS:

210, 353, 415, 727, 894, 959, 964, 3607, 3845

STITCH GUIDE

INSTRUCTIONS:

1 Secure your base fabric with transferred design in your 8cm (3in) embroidery hoop, and get ready to stitch.

2 Work satin stitches for the bunting flags. I have used two strands of thread.

3 Work back stitch for the bunting rope. I have used four strands of thread.

4 Bunting complete! Frame your mini masterpiece.

CLOUD

MATERIALS:

- Fabric, for your base – I have used quilting cotton in white
- 5cm (2¼in) Dandelyne™ miniature embroidery hoop

SUGGESTED STITCHES:

- Back stitch
- Satin stitch

DMC COLOURS:

Blanc, 353, 415, 3845, 964, 3341, 3607

STITCH GUIDE

INSTRUCTIONS:

1 Secure your base fabric with transferred design in your 8cm (3in) embroidery hoop, and get ready to stitch.

2 Work satin stitch to fill the cloud and raindrops. I have used three strands of thread.

3 Work back stitch for the outlines of the cloud and rain drops. I have used three strands of thread.

4 Cloud complete! Frame your mini masterpiece.

EMBELLISH A MOTIF

Hands up if you love fabric, and could spend hours admiring the printed designs? Me too. I enjoy visualizing the possibilities of personalizing my fabric by adding little details here and there. By using printed fabrics you can really let your imagination run wild and make the motifs come alive. Your stitches become an extension of the design. You can choose to follow and highlight the design lines with similar colour threads, or use contrasting colours for a completely different effect. The stitches that you choose will also vary the look. There is absolutely no right or wrong way.

One of the best things about experimenting with printed fabric is the repetition of the design. Yes, you have metres and metres of experimental stitching time. How awesome does that sound?

MATERIALS:

- ❀ Fabric, for your base – choose a printed fabric that tickles your fancy and looks like it would love a little of your embroidery magic added to it
- ❀ Six-stranded embroidery thread, in colours that correspond with your fabrics. You can then split the thread into the number of strands desired
- ❀ Dandelyne™ miniature embroidery hoops of your choice that suit your designs

SUGGESTED STITCHES:

- ❀ Back stitch
- ❀ Running stitch
- ❀ Satin stitch

INSTRUCTIONS:

Detailed instructions are not necessary here because this project is all about letting your imagination and creativity run wild.

My advice is to take your mini hoop and place it on your chosen printed fabric. Move it all around, positioning it in various spots on the fabric until it sits and frames a part of the design that you love. Then, cut out the fabric you need to fit in your 8cm (3in) hoop and start stitching.

❧ DANDE TIP ☙

If you are someone who loves to follow patterns and this appears to be a little overwhelming, remember that the pattern is actually there, on the fabric. Choose corresponding colours and basic stitches for the outline, and then see what happens next. You might find that a little bubble of 'OHMYGOODNESS' pops up in your mind and you see the possibility of adding another feature. Experiment and enjoy!

ABSTRACT IN STITCH

Big, bold and beautiful! Yes! I thought the perfect way to achieve this motto in stitch was with an abstract design. What a statement!

Abstract design, in my eyes, is a wonderful way to express how you might see or feel about a particular thing and represent it in a 'nontraditional' way. When I have time to stitch, it is the style that lights my internal fire. I absolutely love to embroider simple stitches in lots of colours, and in a crazy assortment of shapes. There are no rules and you have the scope to explore and celebrate colour, stitches, design, simplicity and shapes.

Inspiration for abstract design is all around us. In buildings, gift wrapping paper, landscapes, mindful colouring books and faces. The world is open to interpretation and you can stitch it as you see it, not exactly as it is. To create a larger celebration of your design, you can also glue your mini hoops together to make a sublime necklace. Read on...

MATERIALS:

- ❀ Fabric, for your base – I have used quilting cotton in teal and pink
- ❀ Printed fabrics of choice – I have used two with corresponding colours
- ❀ Double-sided fusible web, such as Vliesofix
- ❀ Baking paper
- ❀ Iron
- ❀ **Central design** – 5.5cm (2¼in) Dandelyne™ miniature embroidery hoop
- ❀ **Outer designs** – two 4cm (1½in) Dandelyne™ miniature embroidery hoops

See page 46 for necklace materials.

SUGGESTED STITCHES:

- ❀ Running stitch

DMC COLOURS:

602, 727

INSTRUCTIONS:

1 Cut out your shapes. Here, I have cut semi-circles and strips with a combination of the patterned and plain fabrics.

2 Double-sided fusible web opens yet another door to more possibilities. Just like double-sided tape, but for fabric, you can use it to fuse fabrics together. Cut a piece of double-sided fusible web approx. 10cm (4in) square. Grab your strip and semi-circle and place them on the double-sided fusible web, pattern side facing up. You will then need to cut a piece of baking paper, a little larger than the fusible web, and place it on top. Iron over the baking paper to stick your pieces to the fusible web. Leave it to work its adhesive magic for approx. 10 minutes. Then, peel the baking paper away and cut out your semi-circles and strips. You can then peel off the double-sided fusible web. To do this, use your fingernail to tickle open a corner and then gently peel it off.

3 Lay your pieces on your base fabric. You can use the photograph as a reference for where to place them. Then, iron these onto your fabric, pattern side facing up. Voilà! Now you have two fabrics fused together.

4 Secure your base fabric with ironed-on shapes in your 8cm (3in) embroidery hoop and get ready to stitch.

5 You may choose to follow a similar stitch design to mine; or you can choose to illuminate elements of the pattern in your own fabric. I have used running stitch across the printed pieces. For each colour, I have used three strands of thread.

6 Abstract designs complete. For the central design, frame your mini masterpiece in a 5.5cm (2¼in) Dandelyne™ miniature embroidery hoop; for the outer designs, frame them in 4cm (1½in) Dandelyne™ miniature embroidery hoop. If you wish to make the necklace, don't glue them together yet. Turn over and follow the instructions on page 46...

TEMPLATES

☙ DANDE TIP ☙

A CHALLENGE – draw a few squiggly lines, criss-crossed in a circle of fabric. Next step, choose your favourite colour threads and start filling the spaces with your favourite stitches. Oh, I would absolutely love to see what you've come up with.

Put on your imaginary mini hoop glasses and look around you. What patterns can you see?

NECKLACE MATERIALS:

- *Leather cord – I have used two in different colours*
- *Corresponding-coloured wool, cut to your preferred length*
- *3 x split rings, 8mm – I have used silver*
- *2 x jump rings, 8mm – I have used silver*
- *Parrot clasp, 12mm – I have used silver*
- *Craft wire, 1.02mm (18 gauge)*
- *Flat-nose pliers*
- *Side cutter pliers*
- *Mounting putty (tack)*
- *Industrial strength glue – I use E6000*

HOW TO MAKE THE NECKLACE:

1. Take two strands of leather cord and one strand of different-coloured wool, and loosely plait them together. You can use the photograph on page 45 as a guide.

2. With the pliers, open and attach a split ring to each mini hoop. Close them, and then thread each ringed hoop onto your plaited necklace.

3. Cut a piece of wire, approx. 15cm (6in) long. Fold over one end by approx. 2.5cm (1in), and twist it around itself to leave you with a small loop (as illustrated in the photograph below). Now, holding the wire loop, grab one of your plaited necklace ends and place it just under the loop; begin wrapping the wire around it in a coil (see photo). To make it secure, use your flat-nose pliers to gently squeeze the coil around your strands. Once you're happy it's in place, snip off any excess wire with your side cutter pliers. Repeat for the other end.

4. With your loops secured, attach a jump ring to each one. Attach the parrot clasp to one of these jump rings.

5. With the help of mounting putty (tack), arrange your unglued hoops together in a design that sits perfectly on your chest (and looks terrific too). Hold your necklace up, laying it on your chest to check the positioning of the three hoops together. You can use a pencil to mark where the hoops meet.

6. Using the ever strong E6000 glue, squeeze a small amount of glue on either side of the larger hoop and press the smaller hoops onto it into position. Leave it to dry completely.

7. The result... A magnificent, three-piece, mini hoop masterpiece.

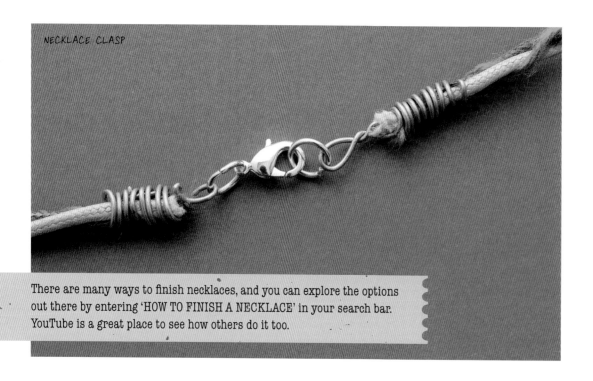

NECKLACE CLASP

There are many ways to finish necklaces, and you can explore the options out there by entering 'HOW TO FINISH A NECKLACE' in your search bar. YouTube is a great place to see how others do it too.

NEON FEATHERS

It's all in the details. So, why not highlight the detail with neon thread? It is so visually effective in appearance that mastering the smooth fibres of this thread will give you an enormous sense of achievement. I promise!

Creating feather designs allows me to admire their beauty and detail at a safe distance, because I am actually a little scared of birds. It is very similar to my inability to keep flowers and plants alive, hence why I absolutely love stitching designs of them.

PEACOCK FEATHER

MATERIALS:

- *Fabric, for your base – I have used quilting cotton in white*
- *Large 3.4 x 6.2cm x ($1\frac{3}{8}$in x $2\frac{1}{2}$in) vertical oval Dandelyne™ miniature embroidery hoop*

SUGGESTED STITCHES:

- *Back stitch*
- *Satin stitch*
- *Straight stitch*

DMC COLOURS:

E980, E990, E1040, E1050, 3809

INSTRUCTIONS:

1. Secure your base fabric with transferred design in your 8cm (3in) embroidery hoop, and get ready to stitch.
2. Use straight stitch to start stitching the main shape and barbs of your feather. I have used one strand of thread.
3. Work satin stitch to fill the central part of the feather. I have used one strand of thread. I like to start in the middle and work my way out. Use the photograph as a reference for colour changes.
4. To finish the design, work back stitches to create the feather shaft and also to frame the central design. I have used one strand of thread.
5. Peacock Feather complete! Frame your mini masterpiece.

STITCH GUIDE

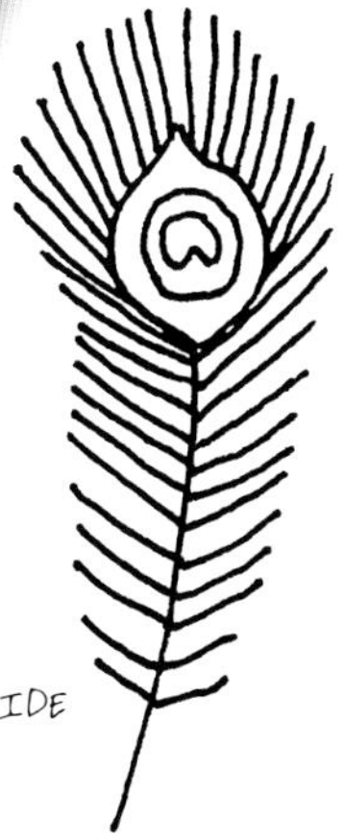

DANDE TIP

I will not lie, neon thread is slippery and tricky to work with. Armed with this knowledge, it is important to work slowly and carefully, and I suggest holding the thread at the eye of the needle throughout so it doesn't slip out. In addition, keep your threads short and if you have thread conditioner, definitely use it – both of these tips will ensure your thread is tangle free and easier to work with.

SINGLE FEATHER

MATERIALS:

❀ Fabric, for your base – I have used quilting cotton in white
❀ Small 2.7 x 4.5cm (1 x 1¾in) vertical oval Dandelyne™ miniature embroidery hoop

SUGGESTED STITCHES:

❀ Straight stitch

DMC COLOURS:

E980, E1010, E1020, E1050

INSTRUCTIONS:

1 Secure your base fabric with transferred design in your 8cm (3in) embroidery hoop, and get ready to stitch.

2 Use straight stitch to start stitching the barbs on your feather. I have used one strand of thread. Use the photograph as a reference for colour changes.

3 To finish your feather off, stitch two straight stitches for the shaft of the feather and approx. six small straight stitches in the top section of the feather, working vertical lines over on alternating barbs to create a couch-like stitch.

4 Single Feather complete. YAY! Frame your mini masterpiece.

STITCH GUIDE

THREE FEATHERS

MATERIALS:

❀ Fabric, for your base – I have used quilting cotton in white
❀ 5.5cm (2¼in) Dandelyne™ miniature embroidery hoop

SUGGESTED STITCHES:

❀ Back stitch
❀ Detached chain stitch
❀ Straight stitch

DMC COLOURS:

E980, E1010, E1020, E1040, 415

INSTRUCTIONS:

1 Secure your base fabric with transferred design in your 8cm (3in) embroidery hoop, and get ready to stitch.

2 Use straight stitch to start stitching your feathers' barbs. I have used one strand of thread. I recommend starting with the two outer feathers and stitching the middle feather last. Use the photograph as a reference for colour changes.

3 Use detached chain stitch for the little feather barbs in the middle and at the top of the central feather (in pink here).

4 To finish the design, work back stitches to create the shafts for your feathers and the outline of the left feather.

5 Three Feathers complete! Frame your mini masterpiece.

STITCH GUIDE

FAMILY PORTRAIT

Guess what? This particular technique was the reason that I started stitching again in 2011. I wanted something a little different from the traditional family photo portrait; so, I thought I should stitch us up (so to speak). I started sketching our family in the way I saw us, in cartoon style, and began creating an embroidered, appliquéd version of us. I was so happy with the result that I showed lots of my friends, and then they wanted one too. It surprised the pants off me. I then began sharing my designs on Instagram and they were a hit. I have stitched hundreds of portraits for beautiful people around the world, and now I get to share this technique with you! Let's stitch up your family and friends.

MATERIALS:

- ❀ Fabric, for your base – I love to use quilting cotton, but you can choose another type that you feel will frame your family and friends in the best light
- ❀ Scraps of plain or printed fabrics of choice, for your family and friends' clothes
- ❀ Small amounts of felt in skin tone shades, for heads or fur
- ❀ Pen or pencil
- ❀ Paper, A4 (8⅓ x 11¾in) in size
- ❀ Double-sided fusible web, such as Vliesofix
- ❀ Baking paper
- ❀ Iron
- ❀ Six-stranded embroidery thread
- ❀ Dandelyne™ miniature embroidery hoop to correspond with your design – my favourite one to use is the 5.5cm (2¼in) size
- ❀ Pins (optional)
- ❀ Clear sticky tape (optional)

SUGGESTED STITCHES:

The stitches you use will be dependant on the look that you are trying to achieve. I like to use straight or satin stitches for straight hair and detached chain stitches for curly hair.

- ❀ Back stitch
- ❀ Detached chain stitch
- ❀ Running stitch
- ❀ Satin stitch
- ❀ Straight stitch

REFERENCE PHOTOS, COURTESY OF BRAD GORDON AND HIS FAMILY

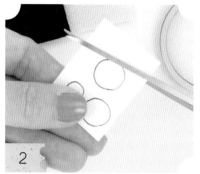

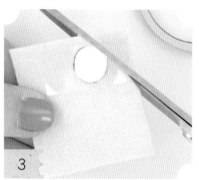

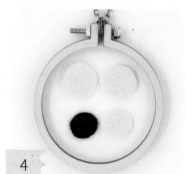

INSTRUCTIONS:

1 First things first. You will need to sketch up your family or friends in a format that you can stitch, and in a Dande-style (see page 51 for examples). You can use a photo as a reference, or work from real life – just remember that these are simple representations of your loved ones, so no intensive details are needed!

With your Dandelyne™ hoop of choice – I am using a 5.5cm (2¼in) hoop – and a pencil, draw a circle onto your fabric using the inner edge of the hoop to create a perimeter for your design. Using your photo (or life models) as a reference, draw circles for the heads in the positions you would like them to appear in your design along with their clothes (you can use the templates provided below right instead, if you prefer). You can then add facial features and hair. You will see that the Dande-style includes a little 'V' for the mouth and two small straight lines for the eyes. This will be your sketch to work from.

2 Using your sketch as a reference or to trace from, create the head templates for your people.

3 With your templates, cut out each head in your chosen felt colour. You can use clear sticky tape to ensure smooth edges on your felt.

4 Once you have cut out all of the heads, place them in your frame to check sizing and placement.

5 Using your felt heads as a reference for size, or your earlier sketch as a guide or to trace from, create clothes templates for your people and cut them out. Place your templates onto their corresponding fabric scraps and cut them out. You can use a pin to hold them in place as you cut, if necessary.

6 Cut a piece of double-sided fusible web, approx. 10cm (4in) square. Grab your clothes and place them on the double-sided fusible web, pattern side facing up. You will then need to cut a piece of baking paper, a little larger than the fusible web, and place it on top. Iron over the baking paper to stick your pieces to the fusible web. Leave it to work its adhesive magic for approx. 10 minutes, then peel away the baking paper and cut out your clothes. You can then peel off the double-sided fusible web; to do this, use your fingernail to tickle open a corner and then gently peel it off.

7 Lay your clothes on your base fabric, using your sketch as a guide for placement. Iron these onto your fabric. Now, you can pop this into your 8cm (3in) embroidery hoop and get ready to stitch.

TEMPLATES

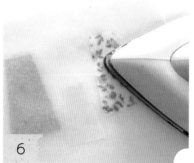

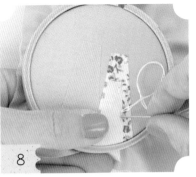  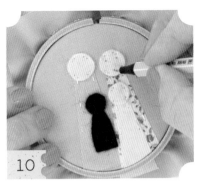

8

9

10

8　Use running stitch to secure the clothes to your base. I like to use stitches approx. 2–3mm (1/8in) in size.

9　Position your felt heads. You can either pin these or simply hold them in place – felt does tend to behave and stay where you like it. Then, stitch your felt heads over your clothes pieces using running stitch. I like to use four stitches, at 2, 4, 8 and 10 o'clock.

10　With your pen, mark the places where you'll stitch the eyes and mouths for your people (and their fur babies), using your earlier sketch as a reference.

11　Stitch your features. Use straight stitches to create the mouth: start at the bottom, in the centre and work in a little 'V'. For the eyes, stitch two small straight stitches.

12　Now for the hair – super fun: start in the middle and work your way out, depending on the hair style. Get messy, keep it tidy, add curls, go wild. Repeat for each person.

Family Portrait complete! Punch the air, high five your friends – YOU HAVE DONE IT! You can now proudly frame in your Dandelyne™ miniature embroidery hoop.

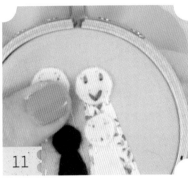

11

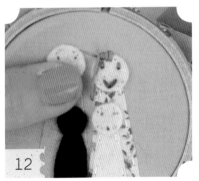

12

🌢 DANDE TIP 🌢

A family portrait may not be complete without your fur babies. You can include them too. Yes you can. Felt heads, felt bodies, stitched ears, whiskers and any other cute little features can all be added.

EMBROIDERY ON LACE

Like many, I enjoy – OK LOVE – entering op shops (charity or thrift shops) in the hope that I will come across a magnificent stash of vintage handkerchiefs, table cloths, doilies and trims. Oh that feeling when you do is gold… I imagine that it is similar to finding out that you have won the lottery. You come home with your winning stash, lay everything out on the kitchen table and high-five yourself for your awesomeness. You then refold everything, very carefully, and place it with all of the many 'wins' you have found or inherited…

So, why not turn them into mini masterpieces and give them a whole new life? What a great idea, if I do say so myself! You could frame them exactly as they are – or add some stitches to highlight their detail and beauty.

MATERIALS:

- Handkerchiefs, table cloths, doilies and trims that you have found or inherited
- Six-stranded embroidery thread, in colours that correspond with your fabrics. You can then split your thread into the number of strands desired
- Dandelyne™ miniature embroidery hoop to correspond with your design

SUGGESTED STITCHES:

I have used:

- Back stitch
- French knot
- Detached chain stitch
- Running stitch
- Satin stitch
- Spider web stitch

INSTRUCTIONS:

The instructions here are very similar to that for the projects on pages 42 to 43 ('Embellish a Motif'), as these projects will be guided by the design of the materials that you are working with. There may be many elements within the pieces that you could embrace and highlight.

Grab your mini hoop and place it on your fabric or trim. Move it all around, positioning it in various spots until it sits and frames a part of the design that you love. Then, cut out the fabric you need to fit in your 8cm (3in) hoop and start stitching. With your fabric's designs already in place, simply add extra floral designs using detached chain stitch or spider web stitch. Add simple stitch lines to enhance the weaves. Possibilities galore!

⁏ DANDE TIP ⁏

There is no rule to say that you can only add flowers or highlight weaves with simple lines. Why not try and stitch a contrasting design to the one on your fabric? You could add a little house, a heart, a feather… and luckily these designs are already created for you, in the templates section for other projects. Oh, now that's an idea…. Mix it up, I say.

SEQUINS & BEADS

Shimmer, sparkle and shine. My love for beads and sequins began as a young girl, when I was learning to dance. I was in awe of the lovely woman who stitched my costumes and I admired the way she stitched with such ease. I would get so excited seeing my costumes come to life so I could bedazzle the audience with my moves and sparkly threads. I remember one particular costume: a one piece, full-body design adorned with blue and green beads and sequins. It made me feel like a magical sea creature. In gratitude to the beautiful woman who made these special clothes, I present to you these sweet sea creatures in all their sparkly glory.

JELLYFISH

STITCH GUIDE

MATERIALS:

- ❀ Fabric, for your base – I have used quilting cotton in blue
- ❀ 5mm sequins – I have used cupped white sequins
- ❀ 1.8mm seed beads – I have used an assortment of pearlescent (pearlized) colours and pastel colours in yellow, peach, pink, white and blue
- ❀ 5.5cm (2¼in) Dandelyne™ miniature embroidery hoop

SUGGESTED STITCHES:

- ❀ Back stitch

DMC COLOURS:

Blanc

❀ DANDE TIP ❀

For these designs I used my regular John James embroidery needle size 5, which worked a treat, but I would recommend using a beading needle because they are more flexible and very thin. The higher the number of the bead, the thinner the needle needs to be.

INSTRUCTIONS:

1 Secure your base fabric with transferred design in your 8cm (3in) embroidery hoop and get ready to stitch.

2 Begin with the jellyfish body. Starting with the right 'ear', back stitch your sequins in place in a sideways-triangle shape. Repeat for the left 'ear'. I have used three sequins. Finish with the main body: starting from the outside and working towards the middle, back stitch in place a spiral of sequins. I have used two strands of thread throughout.

3 Using the photograph as a reference for colour changes, back stitch in place the beads for the jellyfish tentacles. Start at the base of the jellyfish body and work your way down each tentacle. I have used two strands of thread throughout.

4 Now for the beads and sequins at the ends of your tentacles. You will secure these with two stitches. Use the photograph as a reference for placement. Come up through the centre of both the sequin and the bead, and then go over the outside of the bead and back into the fabric through the centre of the sequin. Repeat this once more to ensure the sequin is fastened in place nicely. Continue for the remaining tentacles.

5 Jellyfish complete! Frame your mini masterpiece.

FISHY

STITCH GUIDE

MATERIALS:

- ❀ Fabric, for your base – I have used quilting cotton in aquamarine
- ❀ Scrap of felt, cut to shape and size of the fish head in stitch guide – I have used a mint colour
- ❀ 5mm sequins – I have used flat silver sequins
- ❀ 1.8mm seed beads – I have used an assortment of pearlescent (pearlized) colours and pastel colours in pink, turquoise and mint
- ❀ 4cm (1½in) Dandelyne™ miniature embroidery hoop

SUGGESTED STITCHES:

- ❀ Back stitch
- ❀ Running stitch
- ❀ Straight stitch

DMC COLOURS:

Blanc, E168, 3708, 3842

INSTRUCTIONS:

1 Secure your base fabric with transferred design in your 8cm (3in) embroidery hoop and get ready to stitch.

2 For the fishy head, secure the felt piece with running stitch. Stitch the eyes and mouth with small straight stitches, using the photograph as a reference for placement. I have used two strands of thread.

3 For the beaded sections of your fish's body (see the curved lines on the stitch guide), work back stitch through each bead to secure them in a row, using the photograph as a reference for placement. I have used two strands of thread.

4 For the fins and tail, use back stitch to secure each sequin, using the photograph as a reference for placement. I have used two strands of thread. For the dorsal fin, stitch one sequin flat on the fabric and then stitch the other two sequins so that they slightly overlap the turquoise beads in the centre. These sequins are stitched on one side only.

5 Fishy complete! Frame your mini masterpiece.

STARFISH

STITCH GUIDE

MATERIALS:

- ❀ Fabric, for your base – I have used quilting cotton in mint
- ❀ 5mm sequins – I have used cupped white sequins
- ❀ 1.8mm seed beads – I have used an assortment of pearlescent (pearlized) colours and pastel colours in yellow, peach, pink, white, blue and mint
- ❀ 4cm (1½in) Dandelyne™ miniature embroidery hoop

SUGGESTED STITCHES:

- ❀ Back stitch

DMC COLOURS:

Blanc

INSTRUCTIONS:

1 Secure your base fabric with transferred design in your 8cm (3in) embroidery hoop and get ready to stitch.

2 Use back stitch to secure each sequin (see the large curved lines on the stitch guide). For the fifth and final curve of sequins, continue into the middle of your starfish and create a circle of sequins. I have used two strands of thread.

3 Use back stitch to secure a triangle of sequins in the middle (see triangle on stitch guide). I have used two strands of thread.

4 For the beaded sections on the arms of your starfish (see the smaller curved lines on the stitch guide), use back stitch to secure each bead in a row, using the photograph as a reference for colour and placement. I have used two strands of thread.

4 For the beads on top of the sequins, use back stitch to secure each bead in a row, using the photograph as a reference for placement. I have used two strands of thread. For guidance on how to stitch the beads, see the end of Step 4 of the Jellyfish design (page 56).

5 Starfish complete! Frame your mini masterpiece.

STUFFED HOOPS

Texture, height and pure cushy fun. Let's take our little hoops up a level and give them a whole new purpose. PIN CUSHIONS! What? Yes! You could create a whole range of puffy pin cushions and wear them as rings, brooches or necklaces. This will most certainly ensure your needles are in position and ready to use. It could also mean that you are a walking weapon, so be careful when moving from room to room. And it's time to play with some different fabrics too.

MATERIALS:

❀ Chosen fabric (textured, patterned, printed, vintage, upcycled pieces), measuring 10cm (4in) square
❀ Polyester (fibrefill) stuffing
❀ Six-stranded embroidery thread, in colours that correspond with your fabrics. You can then split your thread into the number of strands desired
❀ Dandelyne™ miniature embroidery hoop to suit your needs, and depending on your fabric and design – I love 25mm (1in) hoops for rings, 4cm (1½in) Dandelyne™ miniature embroidery hoops for brooches and 5.5cm (2¼in) hoops for necklaces. All of these would be handy spots for a pin cushion.

SUGGESTED STITCHES:

❀ Back stitch

INSTRUCTIONS:

To celebrate the textures and designs of fabrics you can choose to frame them exactly as they are or add some stitches, for a personal touch, just the same as the ideas expressed on pages 42 to 43 ('Embellish a Motif'). Here, I have added back stitch to the neon flower wheel design, in blue, and also a small piece of blue felt to the centre (I cheated by using a little craft glue to stick this on!).

STUFFING YOUR DESIGN:

The technique I use to puff up a design is different to the regular way you frame your mini masterpieces. To ensure you get lots of height, let's look at the steps:

1 Position your miniature embroidery hoop on top of the area that you would like to frame. Then, keeping the frame in position, flip your fabric and hoop over so your design is pattern side down.

2 Grab a small amount of stuffing and roll it between your hands. This will help give you an idea of the amount you are going to use. Place your stuffing onto the back side of the fabric, and in the frame. Press it in. Flip the hoop, fabric and stuffing over to check the height and positioning. You can take or add more stuffing, as desired.

(Continued...)

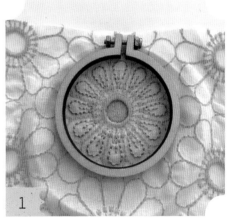

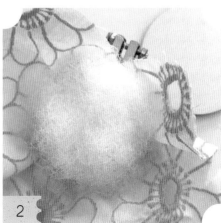

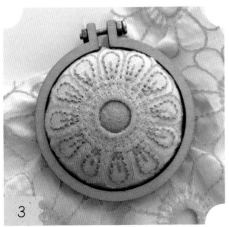

3

3 When you are happy with the height and position, flip your design back over once again and cup it in your hand to help keep the 'puff'. Grab your centre plate and place it on top. Cut off the excess fabric, leaving approx. 7mm (¼in) outside the frame to secure to your centre plate.

4 For the next step, you can keep it in your hand or place it on a table. Use a hot glue gun around the outer edge of the centre plate and gently push your fabric onto the centre piece. Finish framing your design as usual, following the instructions on pages 22–25. As there is stuffing inside, make sure your backing and centre plates are tightly secured while drying, using bull clips or clamps. Your pin cushion is then ready to go!

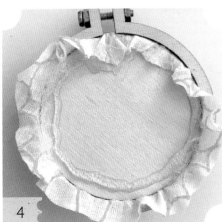

4

HERE, I HAVE MADE AND STITCHED A STUFFED MINI HOOP WITH LIGHT-WEIGHT HESSIAN, USING A TAPESTRY NEEDLE. LESS STUFFING WAS ADDED AS HESSIAN IS QUITE A RIGID FABRIC AND HARDER TO STRETCH, BUT REDUCING THE STUFFING GIVES IT A LOVELY BUTTON-LIKE FINISH. A THICKER THREAD WAS USED, WHICH SUITS THE LARGER WEAVE.

DANDE TIP

If you want to add some puff to other designs in this book, you most definitely can – just use the same instructions as above. If you don't have stuffing on hand, you can make a felt tower: cut small, concentric circles of felt the same circumference as your inner frame, and then pile them on top of one another to achieve the height you desire.

OUTSIDE THE HOOP

Sometimes you just can't keep it all in. Why keep it inside, I say? You can go wild and push the boundaries – literally.

I absolutely love the idea of extending designs beyond the hoop frame. It is perfect for when you want to go bigger, add texture, depth and use different fabrics to illuminate your designs. Felt is a medium that is super fun to use and easy to stitch. I have used it within each of the designs here, illustrating some ways that you could experiment with it too.

DANDE TIP

Thinking outside the hoop opens up a world of fun. Try adding trims such as ribbon, lace, wool or strings of beads to make your mini hoop masterpieces POP. Experiment with thin wire also to help shape the extended features. Another little idea... When stitching some of the family portraits, sometimes I would extend hair plaits outside the hoop, which always looked super cute and effective.

UNICORN

INSTRUCTIONS:

1 With your white felt cut out the unicorn's face and neck, using the templates.

2 Secure your base fabric in your 8cm (3in) embroidery hoop, and get ready to stitch.

3 Position the felt neck onto your basic fabric, followed by the head, and then use running stitch to secure them in place. I have used two strands of thread. You can use pins to secure the felt pieces as you stitch, or just hold them in place. Felt does tend to behave and stay where you want it.

4 Mark the eyes, nostrils, mouth, ears and horn using a pencil, using the photograph as a reference. Then, with corresponding thread, embroider straight stitches onto your unicorn's face to make it come alive. I have used three strands of thread for the eyes and mouth, and one strand for the nostrils. Use satin stitch for the horn. I have used two strands of thread.

5 Next is your unicorn's hair. Eeek... fun! I have used six strands of thread for each colour. I make three stitches, called stem stitches, in every colour; however, I have left them 'unfinished' to create loops which we'll cut through later. Begin with the forehead. Starting with your first colour, come up through the fabric on the far left side of your unicorn's face, near the top of its head. Head back in approx. 2mm (⅛in) to the right of where you started, but don't pull the thread through completely as you want to create a loop. Hold the loop in place with your free hand, and come back up between this stitch to create a second loop **[A]**. Do exactly the same for the third loop **[B]**. Repeat for each shade of thread, working an arch of coloured loops along the top of the head.

6 Return to your first colour once more and follow the same process with the mane, using looped stem stitches all the way down your unicorn's neck.

TIP: A little trick here is to place your mini hoop on top of your design now and then to check that the mane is all going to plan, and will fit within the hoop.

7 Work back stitches along the top of the head and neck to finish off the hair beautifully. I have used two strands of blanc thread.

8 You are now officially a personal unicorn hairdresser. Chop through the loops on that forelock and mane to give your unicorn a beautiful fringe and gorgeous graduated hair down its neck.

9 Unicorn complete! Frame your mini masterpiece.

TEMPLATES

MATERIALS:

❀ *Fabric, for your base – I have used quilting cotton in grey*
❀ *Scrap of white felt*
❀ *Pencil*
❀ *5.5cm (2¼in) Dandelyne™ miniature embroidery hoop*
❀ *Pins (optional)*

SUGGESTED STITCHES:

❀ *Running stitch*
❀ *... and a stitch unique to **Unicorn** project, for its hair: a 'looped' stem stitch*

DMC COLOURS:

Blanc, 169, 210, 307, 602, 809, 959, 964, 3341, 3609, 3845, E3821

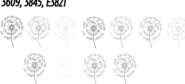

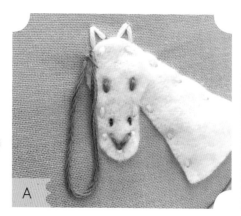

A

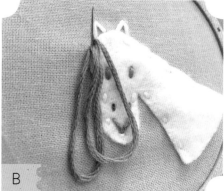

B

HEART BUNTING

MATERIALS:

❧ Fabric, for your base – I have used quilting cotton in white

❧ Scraps of felt in a variety of colours, cut into little hearts – I have used light pink, hot pink, magenta, purple, peach, salmon, orange, yellow, mustard, mint green, green, light blue, turquoise, slate blue and ultramarine (alternatively, scrap pieces that you may have from other projects will come in handy here)

❧ 3 x teardrop beads, white

❧ Pencil

❧ 5.5cm (2¼in) Dandelyne™ miniature embroidery hoop

SUGGESTED STITCHES:

❧ Back stitch

❧ Running stitch

DMC COLOURS:

Perle cotton size 5 in shade 435

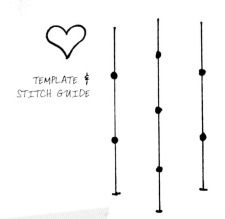

TEMPLATE &
STITCH GUIDE

INSTRUCTIONS:

1 Secure your base fabric with transferred design in your 8cm (3in) embroidery hoop, and get ready to stitch.

2 Work a line of back stitch to create your first bunting string. Place each heart in position as you stitch, using the dots on the stitch guide for reference. When you reach the bottom of your transferred line, leave approx. 10cm (4in) of thread before you snip away the excess – you'll need the length later for your remaining hearts and beads.

   TIP: A little trick here is to place your Dande-hoop on top of your design now and then to check that the hearts are in the right position and to your liking.

3 It's time for a little framing trick. Place your mini hoop frame on top of the design and, before you push it down, gently pull each thread through the hoop. Once all pieces are through, you can then push the hoop down firmly.

4 Flip over your hoop, back facing up; using your hot glue gun, squeeze a line of glue around the edge of the centre plate. Push the fabric down to secure. Flip the hoop back over, ready to attach the extra hearts.

5 Now for the hearts that will hang outside the hoop. Rethreading the first uncut thread, work one running stitch through the centre of one of your remaining hearts and gently tug it into position. Make sure it is relatively equidistant to the previous heart stitched onto your base fabric. Secure the heart with a second running stitch before moving onto the next heart **(A)**. Repeat for the other hearts.

6 Finally, thread and knot a bead at the bottom of each bunting string to give your design a little extra weight, and so the string hangs well and looks fantastic.

7 Heart Bunting complete! Finish framing your mini masterpiece.

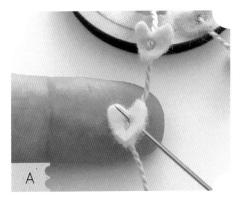

A

❧ DANDE TIP ❧

Cutting out the hearts is a fiddly little job but 100 per cent worth it, I promise. I needed to go back and do a few extra snips to get each heart looking perfect – a little shave off here and there with your fabric scissors works a treat.

STAR BADGE

MATERIALS:

- Fabric, for your base – I have cut 12.7cm (5in) square piece from an A4 (8⅓ x 11¾in) sheet of white felt
- Scraps of white felt (from the sheet) for the ribbon
- Scraps of felt for badge leaves, in a variety of colours – I have used light pink, hot pink, purple, orange, yellow, green, light blue, turquoise, teal and grey (alternatively, scrap pieces that you may have from other projects will come in handy here)
- Pencil
- Tweezers
- 5.5cm (2¼in) Dandelyne™ miniature embroidery hoop
- Pins (optional)

SUGGESTED STITCHES:

- French knots
- Straight stitch

DMC COLOURS:

Blanc, 169, 225, 307, 602, 701, 809, 3609, 3812, 3842, 3845

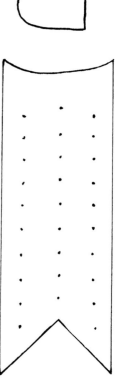

TEMPLATES & STITCH GUIDES

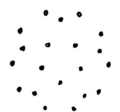

DANDE TIP

For this design, you could stitch without a hoop – felt works well either way.

INSTRUCTIONS:

NOTE: For this project I recommend using one of the transfer methods on page 17, as this will allow you to draw the stitch guides and cut out the pieces for your design more easily.

1 Cut out the badge pieces, using the templates opposite. Using your chosen transfer method on page 17, draw on the stitch guides.

2 With your Dandelyne™ hoop and pencil, draw a circle onto your square piece of felt using the inner edge of the hoop to create a perimeter. This will be a guide for placement of the badge pieces.

3 Secure your felt square with transferred design in your 8cm (3in) embroidery hoop and get ready to stitch.

4 Place your first badge leaf over your drawn circle and secure it at the bottom with one straight stitch. Place your second leaf piece on the line, overlapping your first piece by approx. 2mm (¹⁄₁₆in). Secure this second piece with one straight stitch. Repeat this all the way around, until all badge leaves are in place. I have used two strands of thread throughout.

5 Stitch the star using straight stitch, alternating the colours. I have used three strands of thread.

6 Stitch the points around the frame of the star using French knots, alternating the colours. I have used three strands of thread.

7 Now it's time to make the snazzy felt ribbon. Take your felt ribbon piece cut earlier and work diagonal straight stitches to create the chevrons. Stitch from outer point to the centre point on one side, then repeat on the other. You can tie off each colour on the back **(A)**.

8 Your star badge is nearly complete. Let's start framing it up because I want to share a little trick to get those badge pieces through the hoop... Place your mini hoop frame on top of the design. Just before you push it down, use tweezers to gently pull each piece through the hoop **(B)**. Once all pieces are through you can then continue to push the hoop frame down.

9 Flip it over to the back and with your hot glue gun squeeze a line of glue all the way around the edge of the centre plate. Push the edges of your felt base down to secure your design. Flip the hoop back over to the front and, using your hot glue gun again, squeeze a small line of glue (the same length as the width of the ribbon) at the centre bottom of your hoop frame. Place the top, curved edge of your ribbon onto the glued hoop edge and – hey presto – your Star Badge is now complete. Finish framing your mini masterpiece.

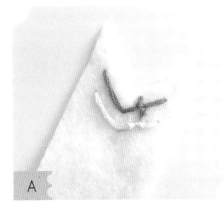

A

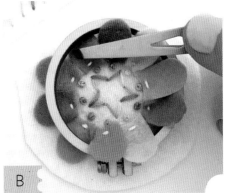

B

CAPTURE A DRAWING

Your children's drawings, a friend's artwork, a precious moment or a memory are just inspiration waiting to be stitched. I love any opportunity to capture these special things, and to be able to wear them close to my heart is a crowning accomplishment. I once stitched my son's first ever drawing, which he fondly titled 'bum-face with one hand' (at the age of four), and it ignites that beautiful memory every time I wear it.

Using my favourite transfer method, with spray adhesive and a photocopier (see page 16), you too have the power to transform many of your precious memories into mini masterpieces. Exciting, huh?

MATERIALS:

- Drawing, sketch or photo that you love or is precious to you
- A4 (8⅓ x 11¾in) sheet of paper
- Pencil
- Paper scissors
- Fabric, for your base – I have used quilting cotton in white
- Polyester (fibrefill) stuffing
- Six-stranded embroidery thread, in colours that correspond with your design. You can then split your thread into the number of strands desired
- Dandelyne™ miniature embroidery hoop to suit your needs, and depending on your fabric and design – I have used a 5.5cm (2¼in) Dandelyne™ miniature embroidery hoop

SUGGESTED STITCHES:

- Back stitch
- Satin stitch
- Straight stitch

INSTRUCTIONS:

1 Once you have chosen a sketch, drawing or photo you will need to create an outline of the design for you to stitch on an A4 (8⅓ x 11¾in) sheet of paper, either by eye or by using one of the methods on pages 16 to 17.

2 Next step is to scale it down to size, to fit in your hoop. You can do this by scanning your image and scaling it down on your computer, by working directly on a photocopier or, again, by eye. Don't worry if it takes two or three attempts to get it to the perfect size.

3 Now it's time to get it onto fabric. For this particular project I would highly recommend using the über-cool method of spray adhesive and a photocopier (see page 16). If you do not have access to a photocopier, you can choose one of the other methods (see page 17) as they will do the trick too.

4 Once your design is transferred, secure your base fabric in your 8cm (3in) embroidery hoop and start stitching. For each of the designs I have used back stitch and one strand of thread for the outlines; for 'colouring-in' I have used a combination of straight stitch and satin stitch, using two strands of thread. When it's complete, frame your mini masterpiece.

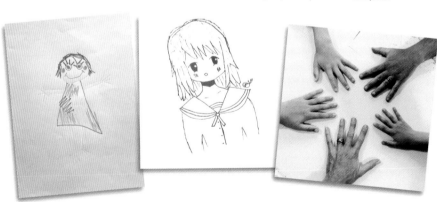

FLORENCE, AGED 7 – LITTLE GIRL DRAWING
MILLY PITT (@EL.ARTSI ON INSTAGRAM) –
BLACK AND WHITE SKETCH
MY FAMILY, THE LYNE FAMILY – HANDS

COUCHING

Oh my sweet crumpets, this delicious stitch is SO. MUCH. FUN. It lends itself to a vast array of designs. You can use couching stitch to hug just about anything. My favourite stitch is reverse chain stitch, but this comes in at a very close second, possibly a tie. And – as the name suggests – you can complete the designs from the comfort of your couch. Couching on the couch. Too much? Heehee.

CELEBRATION OF SCRAPS

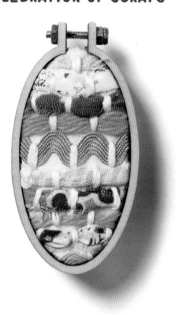

MATERIALS:

❀ Fabric, for your base – I have used quilting cotton in white
❀ Scraps of fabric, threads, yarns and haberdashery in corresponding colours (their length will depend on how thick you'd like your couching to be) – I have used a mixture of fabric, yarn, thread and ric rac
❀ Large 3.4 x 6.2cm x (1⅜ x 2½in) vertical oval Dandelyne™ miniature embroidery hoop

SUGGESTED STITCHES:

❀ Couching

DMC COLOURS:

Blanc

INSTRUCTIONS:

1 Place your scraps on the table in a layout that looks pleasing to your eye. For some of my pieces of fabric, I have rolled them slightly to make them thicker. You can check how your design will look by placing the mini hoop on top. Take a photo for your reference.

2 You may like to pencil in the couch lines on a piece of paper before you begin, to give you an idea of how you want it to look. You can choose to do one stitch, a double stitch, a triple stitch or a cross stitch. Ooooh... Now I've got you thinking.

3 Secure your base fabric in your 8cm (3in) embroidery hoop and get ready to stitch.

4 Position your first piece onto the hoop and couch stitch to secure it in place. Lay your second piece down and use couch stitches to secure it in place, spacing them to form a pattern. Repeat with all the pieces, couch stitching at intervals, until all the scraps are in place.

5 Celebration of Scraps complete! Frame your mini masterpiece.

118   MARY

Regularit
hich is e
any of t

HERRI[NGBON]E STITCH

The working of Close H

Fig. 175

entered for the last crossed
needle is emerging in a sim
the last crossed stitch. The
in order to show the peculi
             parallel rows
             wrong side.
             is worked or
to produce the back stitch
known as Double Back St

SPIRAL

MATERIALS:

- 🌼 Fabric, for your base – I have used quilting cotton in white
- 🌼 Cord – I have used 3mm-thick cord (rope/string/twine)
- 🌼 One 4cm (1½in) and two 2.5cm (1in) Dandelyne™ miniature embroidery hoops

SUGGESTED STITCHES:

- 🌼 Couching
- 🌼 Satin stitch

DMC COLOURS:

353, 602, 809, 959, 964, 3341, 3607, 3608, 3708, 3842, 3845, 3852

INSTRUCTIONS:

1 Start with your 4cm (1½in) size hoop. Secure your base fabric in your 8cm (3in) embroidery hoop and get ready to stitch.

2 I have used six strands of thread for all of the colours. Place the start of your 3mm cotton cord in the centre of your hooped fabric. Beginning with your first thread colour, start couching the cord. This style of stitching is very similar to satin stitch, as you are working the threads closely together. Secure the cord with a few stitches **(A)** and then work back over the beginning of the rope to ensure it is covered entirely.

3 Once you've worked a little of the way round the cord, change your thread colour **(B)**. Repeat this process of couching over the string and changing colour – the number of stitches per colour can be equal in length or different to the previous colour, depending upon your desired outcome.

TIP: The first circle within your spiral may be a little fiddly to manoeuvre and keep in place, but once you've tackled this first round the cord will flow much more easily.

4 As you work, use your mini hoop to check that the spiral is going to plan and will fit within the hoop. Stop stitching when you are happy with the size. Cut the cord on an angle, tapering off to create a smooth circle, and stitch it down.

5 Spiral complete! Or is it? You may like to stitch this again to make earrings, a brooch or keyring. For now, frame your mini masterpiece in a 4cm (1½in) Dandelyne™ miniature embroidery hoop. Then go again!

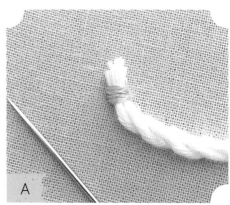

A

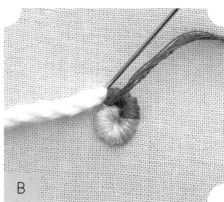

B

TOTEM BAR

MATERIALS:

❀ Fabric, for your base – I have used quilting cotton in pink
❀ 5.5cm (2¼in) Dandelyne™ miniature embroidery hoop

SUGGESTED STITCHES:

❀ Couching
❀ Satin stitch

DMC COLOURS:

225, 353, 958, 964, 3607

INSTRUCTIONS:

1 Secure your base fabric with transferred design in your 8cm (3in) embroidery hoop and get ready to stitch.

2 Using the photograph and stitch guide as references for colour changes, work couch stitch for the 'totem' sections of the design. I have used three strands of thread throughout. For each horizontal line I have varied the couching stitches by placing them at different distances to one another, and working extra stitches to make them look thicker.

3 Using the photograph and stitch guide as references for colour changes, work horizontal satin stitches across the vertical bar down the middle. I have used three strands of thread.

4 Totem Bar complete! Frame your mini masterpiece.

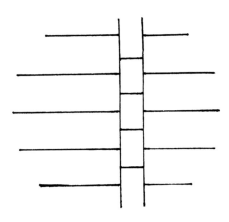

STITCH GUIDE

> ❧ **DANDE TIP** ❧
>
> I get excited at the thought of what you can do with couching stitch. It looks terrific when used in abstract designs, and it can also be very effective as a filling stitch or outline stitch for more realistic designs, such as houses, animals and more. Try using this wonderful stitch with one of the designs from the other projects to give it a whole new look.

METALLIC SASHIKO

'Sashiko' means 'little stabs'. The simplicity of the running stitch used in sashiko's repeated geometric patterns is awe-inspiring. There are rules for this beautiful craft, and what I love and respect is that the stitches should be of equal lengths in order to create an elegant and clean look.

The designs that I have used here are common sashiko patterns, with a shiny twist. Using only a single strand of metallic thread, you can enjoy stitching a mini sashiko design – or three. Here we go!

CIRCLES

MATERIALS:

❁ Fabric, for your base – I have used quilting cotton in magenta
❁ 5.5cm (2¼in) Dandelyne™ miniature embroidery hoop

SUGGESTED STITCHES:

❁ Running stitch

DMC COLOURS:

E3821

INSTRUCTIONS:

1 Secure your base fabric with transferred design in your 8cm (3in) embroidery hoop and get ready to stitch.

2 Work running stitches for the entire design. I have used one strand of thread.

3 Circles complete! Frame your mini masterpiece.

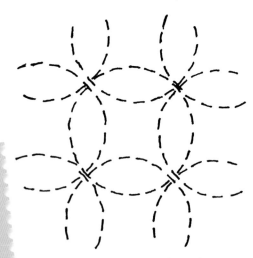

STITCH GUIDE

❧ DANDE TIP ❧

Exploring the art, you will find that there are four key materials that are fundamental for sashiko: special sashiko needles (which are extra long), thread, thimble and fabric. The running stitch used in traditional sashiko is worked using the so-called 'sewing method', whereby you run your needle in and out of the fabric, scooping it for several stitches, before finally pulling the thread through. The 'stab method' of taking your needle and thread to the back of the fabric and bringing it to the front again is the other technique commonly used. Feel free to use either technique for these designs.

The history of sashiko embroidery is truly captivating and I highly encourage you to search and read up on this mesmerizing art. A little warning: you may get lost in the designs and techniques for hours.

CUBES

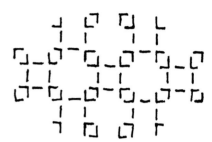

MATERIALS:

❀ Fabric, for your base – I have used quilting cotton in cornflower blue
❀ Large 6.2 x 3.4cm (2½ x 1⅜in) horizontal oval Dandelyne™ miniature embroidery hoop

SUGGESTED STITCHES:

❀ Running stitch

DMC COLOURS:

E168

INSTRUCTIONS:

1 Secure your base fabric with transferred design in your 8cm (3in) embroidery hoop, and get ready to stitch.

2 Work running stitches for the entire design. I have used one strand of thread.

3 Cubes complete! Frame your mini masterpiece.

FANS

MATERIALS:

❀ Fabric, for your base – I have used quilting cotton in aquamarine
❀ 4cm (1½in) Dandelyne™ miniature embroidery hoop

SUGGESTED STITCHES:

❀ Running stitch

DMC COLOURS:

S352

INSTRUCTIONS:

1 Secure your base fabric with transferred design in your 8cm (3in) embroidery hoop, and get ready to stitch.

2 Work running stitches for the entire design. I have used one strand of thread.

3 Fans complete! Frame your mini masterpiece.

VINTAGE FLORALS

What do you get when you combine classic fabrics with vintage-inspired embroidered designs? In my eyes, symbiosis!

Linen; oh, divine linen. I remember ironing linen table cloths for my mum and feeling so satisfied as each crease was smoothed out. Denim is a material that has been in my life since I can remember (denim jeans!), and my memories of gingham go back to my wearing school uniforms and learning to embroider: we were given gingham squares to practise our stitches and stitch lengths. It worked a treat.

Let's celebrate what has been gifted to us from our crafty ancestors, wrap it up in a mini hoop and shout THANK YOU!

BASKET OF FLOWERS

STITCH GUIDE

MATERIALS:

❀ Fabric, for your base – I have used linen in oatmeal
❀ Large 3.4cm x 6.2 cm (1⅜ x 2½in) vertical oval Dandelyne™ miniature embroidery hoop

SUGGESTED STITCHES:

❀ Back stitch
❀ Detached chain stitch
❀ Satin stitch
❀ Straight stitch

DMC COLOURS:

225, 554, 602, 840, 3347

INSTRUCTIONS:

1 Secure your base fabric with transferred design in your 8cm (3in) embroidery hoop, and get ready to stitch.

2 Work back stitches to make the main shape and outline of the basket. I have used three strands of thread.

3 Use satin stitch to create the handle of the basket. I have used three strands of thread.

4 To take it up a notch you are now going to whip your back stitch for the outline of the basket. Using two strands of thread and starting from the top left of your basket outline, swoop your needle over to the right side of the stitch and come out on the left, literally wrapping the thread around it. Repeat all the way around.

5 Work straight stitches for the weave of the basket. I have used one strand of thread. Stitch single, long straight stitches for the diagonals that are slanting down to the right, and then repeat for the diagonals slanting down to the left, stitching them over the top. Basket complete.

6 Now for the flowers. Work back stitches for stems of the grasses. I have used two strands of thread.

7 Work detached chain stitches for the leaves. I have used two strands of thread.

8 Using the photograph as a reference to colour changes, work satin stitch for the centres. I have used two strands of thread. For the centres, I have worked the stitches in one direction and then, for the petals, radiated the stitches around the centres.

9 Basket of Flowers complete! Frame your mini masterpiece.

♪ DANDE TIP ♪

If you have vintage pieces that have been gifted to you, or have found sweet pieces in op shops (charity shops or thrift stores) and you're not sure what to do with them, you could use a section of the design and frame it up in a mini hoop exactly as it is – no stitching required, and a chance to celebrate its beauty.

LAVENDER

MATERIALS:

- Fabric, for your base – I have used denim
- Length of ribbon, approx. 10cm (4in) long x 3–4mm (⅛in) wide
- 5.5cm (2¼in) Dandelyne™ miniature embroidery hoop

SUGGESTED STITCHES:

- Back stitch
- French knots

DMC COLOURS:

210, 225, 552, 701

INSTRUCTIONS:

1. Secure your base fabric with transferred design in your 8cm (3in) embroidery hoop, and get ready to stitch.

2. Work back stitch for the lavender stems. I have used two strands of thread.

3. Using the photograph as a reference for colour changes, stitch French knots for the lavender buds. I have used two strands of thread.

4. For the ribbon: tie a little bow and secure it in place by wrapping stitches around the centre in corresponding coloured thread. Effectively, you are using couch stitch here. I have used two strands of thread.

5. Lavender complete! Frame your mini masterpiece.

STITCH GUIDE

COLOURFUL DAISIES

MATERIALS:

- Fabric, for your base – I have used gingham in yellow and white
- Large 3.4cm x 6.2cm (1⅜ x 2½in) vertical oval Dandelyne™ miniature embroidery hoop

SUGGESTED STITCHES:

- Back stitch
- Detached chain stitch
- French knots

DMC COLOURS:

Blanc, 225, 353, 809, 3328, 3347

INSTRUCTIONS:

1. Secure your base fabric with transferred design in your 8cm (3in) embroidery hoop, and get ready to stitch.

2. First, work back stitches for the stems of the flowers. I have used two strands of thread.

3. Use detached chain stitch for the leaves on the stems. I have used two strands of thread.

4. Work detached chain stitches for the flower petals. I have used two strands of thread.

5. Stitch French knots for the centre of your flowers. I have used one strand of thread.

6. Colourful Daisies complete! Frame your mini masterpiece.

STITCH GUIDE

WOOLLY FUN

Crewel embroidery is the term applied when using wool as a medium. Fun, yes?

The texture and boldness that wool gives a design excites me to the nth degree. Using embroidery stitches and inspiration from all things created from wool, I have designed three pieces that I am sure will tickle your fancy. I have incorporated a little macramé and weaving to get your stitchy fingers moving. Are you with me? Let's dive in!

RAYS OF SUN

MATERIALS:

❀ Fabric, for your base – I have used linen in natural colour

❀ Wool type of choice – I have used 100% pure wool in hot pink, mustard, orange and teal

❀ 5.5cm (2¼in) Dandelyne™ miniature embroidery hoop

SUGGESTED STITCHES:

❀ Straight stitch

INSTRUCTIONS:

1 Secure your base fabric with transferred design in your 8cm (3in) embroidery hoop, and get ready to stitch.

2 Using the photograph as a reference for colour changes, enjoy working the simple straight stitches needed to create each ray.

   TIP: You can also create different colourways for your own sun by alternating colours, using less or more of one colour, or even deviating from wool altogether and working in a few strands of metallic embroidery thread.

3 Rays of Sun complete! Frame your mini masterpiece.

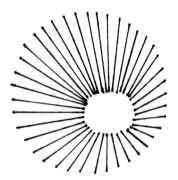

STITCH GUIDE

CRISS-CROSS WEAVE

MATERIALS:

❀ Fabric, for your base – I have used linen in natural colour
❀ Wool type of choice – I have used navy, teal and hot pink
❀ 4cm (1½in) Dandelyne™ miniature embroidery hoop

SUGGESTED STITCHES:

❀ Straight stitch

INSTRUCTIONS:

1 Secure your base fabric with transferred design in your 8cm (3in) embroidery hoop, and get ready to stitch.

2 For this design you will use straight stitch to create the grid. The grid will also become your weaves. I have used navy wool for the vertical lines and hot pink wool for the horizontal lines. Begin with the vertical lines, working large straight stitches for each line. Then, to create the weave, work straight stitches horizontally and weave them over and under the vertical lines. After your first row of weaving, finish the straight stitch and come back up through the fabric again at the beginning of your second row to start this line of weaving. Make sure that you go over and under in the opposite direction to the previous row.

3 Now it's time to couch the grid into position. I have used teal wool for this stitch. Using the photograph as a guide, work small straight stitches at an angle over alternate horizontal and vertical intersections.

4 Criss-Cross Weave complete! Frame your mini masterpiece.

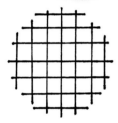

STITCH GUIDE

⸮ DANDE TIP ⸮

I am certain if wool could speak it would say 'Please make at least one pompom out of me.' You can do just that by using the same method for the unicorn mane on page 64 ('Outside the Hoop') – TRY IT!

MINI MACRAMÉ

MATERIALS:

- Fabric, for your base – *I have used linen in natural colour*
- Wool type of choice – *I have used mustard, magenta and turquoise*
- Pencil or fabric pen
- *Large 3.4cm x 6.2cm (1⅜ x 2½in) vertical oval Dandelyne™ miniature embroidery hoop*

SUGGESTED STITCHES:

- *Straight stitch*
- *Couch stitch*

DMC COLOURS:

415

INSTRUCTIONS:

This design may vary slightly depending upon the thickness of the wool that you have chosen. My instructions are for the design illustrated; however, if you find that you would like to work more or work less couching, or create more or fewer macramé knots, go wild.

1 Secure your base fabric in your 8cm (3in) embroidery hoop and get ready to stitch and knot.

2 Using your mini hoop, trace the inner edge of the frame with your pencil or fabric pen as a guide for size. Then, place your first strands of wool at the top of the circle. I have used two strands. With two strands of your embroidery thread, couch stitch over the wool to secure them into position. Repeat for the next two wool colours. You can see in the photograph that, with the third colour, the wool I used was thicker and required additional couch stitches to secure them in place.

3 Now... macramé knot time. YAY! Stitch one straight stitch directly below your last couch stitch and secure it at the back by tying the ends together **(A)**. This straight stitch will be the base for your macramé knots.

4 Cut six lengths of wool approx. 12cm (5in) long – I have used a mustard colour. Cut a piece of embroidery thread to the same length – I have used two strands of DMC 415. You should have seven pieces in total to knot.

5 Fold each piece of wool in half. With your first piece of wool, slide the loop over the straight stitch; once it's over, open up the loop and thread the ends of your wool through it **(B)**. Pull until you have your knot. Voilà! Repeat for each strand **(C)**. In between the six folded strands of wool, you'll see I have knotted embroidery thread in the same way as the wool, to add interest at the centre of the design.

6 Stitch your second straight stitch approx. 1cm (¼in) under your last straight stitch to begin your second row of macramé knots. With seven pieces of the same coloured wool, follow Steps 4 and 5. Repeat once more for the third and final row.

TIP: I recommend placing your mini hoop on top of your design now and then as you work, to check that everything is fitting and to your liking. Feel free to add or remove elements of the design to make it just right.

7 Mini Macramé complete! Frame your mini masterpiece.

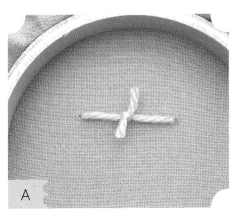

A

B

C

MONOGRAM

Simple and super effective! You can stitch an initial, a word or a phrase and it speaks volumes.

I have stitched many letters of the alphabet for gifts, and they have all been warmly received. An 'initial' mini hoop could be worn close to the heart as a necklace or brooch, and it could also be transformed into a keyring to hang off your bag or car keys.

Below are some ideas for you to try using 'M', 'S' and 'A'. You can use the same instructions to stitch any letter, number or symbol you like, using the templates on page 87.

LETTER 'M'

MATERIALS:
- Fabric, for your base – I have used quilting cotton in magenta
- 4cm (1½in) Dandelyne™ miniature embroidery hoop

SUGGESTED STITCHES:
- Back stitch
- French knots
- Running stitch
- Straight stitch

DMC COLOURS:
225, 3607

INSTRUCTIONS:

1 Secure your base fabric with transferred initial (see page 87) in your 8cm (3in) embroidery hoop and get ready to stitch.

2 Work a circle of running stitches to create a frame for your initial. I have used one strand of thread.

3 Work back stitch to stitch the 'M'. I have used two strands of thread.

4 Use straight stitch to complete the three lines in the middle of the 'M'. I have used one strand of thread.

5 Work French knots at the top of the 'M'. I have used one strand of thread.

6 Use cross stitch (two straight stitches) to complete the crosses on the background.

7 'Letter 'M' complete! Frame your mini masterpiece.

⁑ DANDE TIP ⁑

The font that I have used (see page 87) is fun to play with and lends itself to being stitched in a variety of ways. You can choose to stitch the outline, fill in your letter and add some extra stitches for a personal touch.

LETTER 'S'

MATERIALS:

- Fabric, for your base – I have used quilting cotton in pink
- 4cm (1½in) Dandelyne™ miniature embroidery hoop

SUGGESTED STITCHES:

- Back stitch
- French knots
- Satin stitch

DMC COLOURS:

959, 964

INSTRUCTIONS:

1 Secure your base fabric wth transferred initial (see page 87) in your 8cm (3in) embroidery hoop and get ready to stitch.

2 Fill the shape of the 'S' with satin stitch. I have used two strands of thread.

3 Use back stitch to create the outline of the 'S'. I have used two strands of thread.

4 Work French knots next to the top left curve of the 'S'. I have used one strand of thread.

5 Letter 'S' complete! Frame your mini masterpiece.

LETTER 'A'

MATERIALS:

- Fabric, for your base – I have used aqua cotton with a geometric print
- 4cm (1½in) Dandelyne™ miniature embroidery hoop

SUGGESTED STITCHES:

- French knots
- Reverse chain stitch
- Straight stitch

DMC COLOURS:

602

INSTRUCTIONS:

1 Secure your base fabric with transferred initial (see page 87) in your 8cm (3in) embroidery hoop and get ready to stitch.

2 Work a curved line of reverse chain stitch to create the main shape of the 'A'. I have used two strands of thread.

3 Use straight stitch to make the three lines in the middle of 'A'. I have used one strand of thread.

4 Work French knots in the 'eye' of your 'A'. I have used one strand of thread, but wrapped the thread around the needle once more to create the chunkier French knots.

5 Letter 'A' complete! Frame your mini masterpiece.

ABCDEFGHIJK
LMNOPQRSTU
VWXYZ

abcdefghijklmn
opqrstuvwxyz
&!%$#@
0123456789

Note: For multiple characters, you may need to re-size on your photocopier/printer's scanner.

PET BLING

I may have squealed with excitement when I designed the accessories for these cute little fur babies. Using the photographs here, or of your own pets, and the wonderful transfer method of 'spray and print' (see page 16), you can transform any photo into something truly unique.

Once you have chosen a photo, you will need to scale it down to size to fit in your hoop. You can do this by scanning your photo on your printer and scaling it down on your computer, or do it directly on a photocopier. It may take two or three attempts to get it to the perfect size. You then transfer your picture to the fabric with the 'spray and print' method.

PIGGY

MATERIALS:

❀ Fabric, for your base – I have used quilting cotton in white
❀ 5.5cm (2¼in) Dandelyne™ miniature embroidery hoop

SUGGESTED STITCHES:

❀ Back stitch
❀ Reverse chain stitch
❀ Satin stitch

DMC COLOURS:

Blanc, 225, 894, 964, 3607, 3842, 3852

INSTRUCTIONS:

1 Secure your base fabric with transferred photo in your 8cm (3in) embroidery hoop and get ready to stitch.

2 Using the photograph on this page as a reference for colour changes and placement, work reverse chain stitch for the beanie stripes on your piggy's hat. I have stitched two rows of reverse chain stitch for the cuff of the beanie, and then used single rows of reverse chain stitch for the rest of the beanie. I have used one strand of thread for each colour.

   TIP: When you have finished a row/stripe, take your needle from the back through to the front at the tip of the beanie, leaving a little extra thread before you snip; this is so you can create and snip into shape the tiny pompom at the end of your hat.

3 Using the photograph as a reference for colour changes and placement, work satin stitch for the mittens. I have used two strands of thread.

4 Use back stitch to frame the shape of the beanie and mittens. I have used one strand of thread.

5 Snip the threads at the tip of the piggy's beanie for a cute little pompom.

6 Piggy complete! Frame your mini masterpiece.

PHOTO TO USE
FOR TRANSFER

❀ **DANDE TIP** ❀

When choosing some accessories and bling for your pets think about dress up costumes, themes, seasons and occasions; then, let your imagination run wild.

BULLDOG

MATERIALS:

❀ Fabric, for your base – I have used quilting cotton in white
❀ 5.5cm (2¼in) Dandelyne™ miniature embroidery hoop

SUGGESTED STITCHES:

❀ Back stitch
❀ Satin stitch
❀ Straight stitch

DMC COLOURS:

310

INSTRUCTIONS:

1 Secure your base fabric with transferred photo in your 8cm (3in) embroidery hoop and get ready to stitch.

2 Use back stitch to make the glasses frame and collar for the bow tie. I have used one strand of thread.

3 Use satin stitch to create the shape of the bow tie. I have used one strand of thread.

4 Use straight stitches to frame each side of the bow tie triangles. I have used one strand of thread.

5 Bulldog complete! Frame your mini masterpiece.

PHOTO TO USE FOR TRANSFER

LAUGHING CAT

MATERIALS:

❀ Fabric, for your base – I have used quilting cotton in white
❀ 5.5cm (2¼in) Dandelyne™ miniature embroidery hoop

SUGGESTED STITCHES:

❀ Back stitch
❀ French knots
❀ Satin stitch
❀ Straight stitch

DMC COLOURS:

Blanc, 307, 321, 907, 3845

INSTRUCTIONS:

1 Secure your base fabric with transferred photo in your 8cm (3in) embroidery hoop and get ready to stitch.

2 Work straight stitch for the ruffles in the clown collar. Then, in a separate colour, use back stitch to frame the frill at the top. I have used one strand of thread for both colours.

3 Use satin stitch to make the red nose for your cat. I have used one strand of thread.

4 Using the photograph on this page as a reference for colour and colour changes, stitch French knots for your cat's crazy hair. I have used one strand of thread.

5 Laughing Cat complete! Frame your mini masterpiece.

PHOTO TO USE FOR TRANSFER

GEOMETRIC PATTERNS

The creative results that you can achieve by simply arranging shapes in a variety of ways is endless. If you look around your space right now, I am certain that you will see patterns everywhere... A display of objects on a shelf, on your bookcase, a windowsill, or even in the way your dishes are stacked in a sink (although it may be messy, there is still a design in there). Put your imaginary mini hoop glasses on and sketch a few of the patterns that you see. Look at your sketches, and then reimagine each section in your favourite stitches. Voilà – an instant design.

Wonderful artists do this and share their designs on fabric. You can utilize the beauty of your subjects' forms and transform the patterns on them into a different geometric design, just by adding a line or a shape.

BLOCKS STACKED

MATERIALS:

❀ Fabric, for your base – I have used quilting cotton in purple
❀ 5.5cm (2¼in) Dandelyne™ miniature embroidery hoop

SUGGESTED STITCHES:

❀ Back stitch
❀ Couch stitch
❀ French stitch
❀ Reverse chain stitch
❀ Running stitch
❀ Satin stitch
❀ Straight stitch

DMC COLOURS:

415, 727, 809, 958, 3341, 3607, 3708

INSTRUCTIONS:

1 Secure your base fabric with transferred design in your 8cm (3in) embroidery hoop and get ready to stitch.

2 You can start on this design wherever your heart desires! The list below is the order in which I stitched. Use the photograph and stitch guide as references for colour changes and placement of stitches:

   A. Running stitch (two strands of thread)
   B. Back stitch (three strands of thread)
   C. Satin stitch (two strands of thread)
   D. Reverse chain stitch (two strands of thread)
   E. Couching (three strands of thread)
   F. French knots (one strand of thread).

3 Blocks Stacked complete! Frame your mini masterpiece.

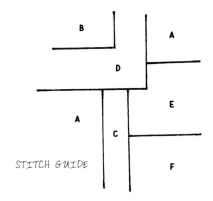

STITCH GUIDE

WHERE PINK & MINT MEET

MATERIALS:

❀ Fabric, for your base – I have used cotton drill with a striped pattern
❀ 4cm (1½in) Dandelyne™ miniature embroidery hoop

SUGGESTED STITCHES:

❀ Straight stitch

DMC COLOURS:

964, 3609

INSTRUCTIONS:

1 Secure your base fabric with transferred design in your 8cm (3in) embroidery hoop and get ready to stitch.

2 Using the photograph as a reference for colour changes, work straight stitches to create small to large chevrons. Work from the outside inwards, working on the left side first and then on the right. I have used three strands of thread.

3 Where Pink & Mint Meet complete! Frame your mini masterpiece.

STITCH GUIDE

DIAMOND

STITCH GUIDE

MATERIALS:

❀ Fabric, for your base –I have used printed cotton with a diamond pattern
❀ 2.5cm (1in) Dandelyne™ miniature embroidery hoop

SUGGESTED STITCHES:

❀ Straight stitch

DMC COLOURS:

E168

INSTRUCTIONS:

1 Secure your base fabric with transferred design in your 8cm (3in) embroidery hoop and get ready to stitch.

2 Use straight stitch to create your diamond. I have used one strand of thread.

3 Diamond complete! Frame your mini masterpiece.

❀ DANDE TIP ❀

Geometric printed fabric is widely available and just waiting for some extra stitches to be added to it. The simplicity of a few lines can be transformed into so many shapes. You can use the designs on the fabric to simply colour in, outline or highlight what is already there.

ACKNOWLEDGEMENTS

This is a very important part of the book for me and I feel like I could be on a stage accepting a Golden Globe Award (hahaha), because honestly, I am beyond grateful for everyone in my life that supports and encourages me to follow my passion, who never let me give up and who help me strive towards all of my embroidery dreams. So, to start in a true Hollywood awards style, I want to say an ENORMOUS thank you.

This book would not have been possible without:

Our crafty ancestors – to the many who have passed down their needlepoint skills through generations, I am forever in your debt. It is an honour to indulge in every single stitch and I continually feel a huge sense of connection and gratefulness.

All of my hoopie Instagram community/friends – you have been with me on this Dande-ride and oh, what a ride! I never want to get off. It is because of each and every one of you that I feel I can always push myself just that little more. Each of your comments, emails and all round love oozes through my screens, and although we may not have met I most definitely call you my friends, my stitchy sisters/bros, and the backbone of why I do what I do. Thank you for your enthusiasm, your mini hoop art and investing in Dandelyne™ hoops too. You all continually inspire me.

Emily, Katie, Maz and the entire team at Search Press – oh my sweet crumpets, Katie and Emily; I am incredibly grateful to you both. Your ideas, vision, guidance and skills have meant that I have been able to produce a book that I am above and beyond proud of.

Thank you for gifting me this opportunity to express my heart in a book. The end result has exceeded my expectations, and then some. When you visit Australia, I would love for you to come and visit so I can give you the biggest squeezes.

Stacy Grant, the photographer – WOW! You have illuminated my little hoops in a way that has left me speechless. I promise, that never happens. To the moon and back, and around and around, thank you.

My Dande-team… Tom, Jenni and Gabriel – you are most definitely the best team a kooky girl like me could ever ask for, and you know that I ask a lot. You bring my passion to life with every detail and through every crazy request. I am proud to call you my friends, and your support of what I do means more than I know how to express.

Mrs Carol Mulrooney – the amazing woman who was my very first embroidery teacher. I have the fondest memories of learning to embroider on gingham squares in our Uranquinty P.S. library, and I remember wanting to impress the pants off you. Little did you know, or I at the time, that those first few stitches lit an internal fire that now burns like a wild bush fire.

My friends – I was once told that you would be able to count your true friends on one hand. I am one lucky lady, because I started to count and I didn't have enough fingers and toes. You are all my biggest cheerleaders and my family, and I cannot imagine a life without your words of wisdom, laughs, coffees, champagne and all round support. I just tried then… nope, no way!

My brothers, sister and extended families – Carl, Tania and Brad; my adopted mums and dads, Barb and Wal, Barry and Wendy, Helen and Adrian, Joy and Diz, Ma and Gra; and, of course, Mum and Dad. Thank you for guiding me and showing me how to be the best version of myself. Each of you have had a significant impact on my life at different times, and helped me path a direction that I am so proud of. I love you and your generous hearts.

My family – Alex, Phoenix, Anderson, Austin and Falkor. I have saved the best for last because REALLY, yep, REALLY my world is SO MUCH BETTER because each of you are in it. As I always say, 'I flippin' love the heck out of all of you!' I promise to keep following my dreams, your dreams, our dreams... so that together we create a life that we are all so proud of! Your support, encouragement, laughter, crazy ideas, pretend happiness over some of my dodgy meals, arguments and plans for adventures complete me.

Dandelyne™ has given me a worldwide community that I adore. Words cannot describe how grateful I am for this. The only way that I know how to say thank you to the best community in the world is to continue stitching, continue to make the best little hoops in the world and continue to follow my passion: all things embroidery. For all of this I am grateful. EVERY. SINGLE. DAY.